REAL·H   S
of the
SOUTH WEST

Pub Interiors of Special Historic Interest

Edited by **Paul Ainsworth, Russ Durbridge** and **Michael Slaughter**

With photography by Michael Slaughter LRPS and Michael Schouten

CAMRA BOOKS

Based on CAMRA's South West Regional Inventory of Historic Pub Interiors

Produced by CAMRA's Pub Heritage Group
www.heritagepubs.org.uk
info.pubheritage@camra.org.uk

For CAMRA Books
Managing Editor: Katie Button
Sales and Marketing: Toby Langdon

Book design/typography: Dale Tomlinson
Maps: Alejandra Gutierrez

Published by the Campaign for Real Ale Ltd.
230 Hatfield Road, St Albans
Hertfordshire AL1 4LW
www.camra.org.uk/books

© Campaign for Real Ale Ltd 2019

First published 2019

ISBN 978-1-85249-361-5

A CIP catalogue record for this book is available from
the British Library

Printed and bound in the United Kingdom by
Cambrian Printers Ltd, Aberystwyth

PHOTO CREDITS

The majority of the photographs are by
Michael Slaughter, with a considerable number
by Michael Schouten and are indicated in the
caption by (MSS). Other photos were supplied
by Tim Belsten, Geoff Brandwood, Mark Finney
and Yanai Sharabi and are acknowledged
accordingly where they appear.

Cover: (*Front*) The Plough at Prestbury,
Gloucestershire; (*Back*) Black Horse,
Clapton-in-Gordano, Somerset

Title page: Cash register handpumps at the
Old Crown, Kelston, Somerset

This page: (*top*) Public Bar window, Cricketers,
Bournemouth, Dorset; (*below*) Lounge window,
Victoria Hotel, Oldfield Park, Bath, Somerset

Contents

Introduction   **Pubs to Cherish**

Real Heritage Pubs of the South West celebrates 109 pub interiors in South West England which CAMRA has identified as having special historic interest. They represent an important aspect of the area's cultural and built heritage, with quite a number being true national treasures.

That said, they account for only 2% or so of the pubs in the area – why is this so? A major reason, of course, is that pub interiors have always been subject to change. The only pubs that are exactly the same as the day they opened are ones which came into being in the last few years. The pace of change, though, accelerated dramatically from the 1960s. At that time, a mania began for opening out, faddish theming, image change and general trashing. Consequently, many pubs suffered makeovers during which most, if not all, vestiges of original or early features were lost.

The irony is that interest in historic buildings has never been greater. Lots of us are fascinated by our built heritage and spend time visiting historic buildings of many kinds. It is, though, only in recent years – and largely as a result of CAMRA's efforts – that pub interiors have come to be valued by mainstream conservationists. CAMRA picked up the baton on behalf of our pub heritage, filling the gaps in knowledge of what is out there and actively seeking to protect what is left. It has worked closely with Historic England (formerly known as English Heritage) to gain statutory protection through the listing process for the most important examples we have identified. Nonetheless, losses still happen, either through closure or changes by insensitive owners eager to tear them apart.

This is the ninth and penultimate in a series of regional guides to our best heritage pubs and draws on many years of work by CAMRA members to track down and record those that have escaped the attention of the modernisers and 'improvers'. We hope it will help increase awareness of their importance. Enjoy your visits.

The Haunch of Venison, Salisbury showing the tiny snug, pewter bar top and rare set of spirit cocks

What Shaped Pubs in the South West

Is there such a thing as a 'typical' South West pub? Given the large and varied nature of the region and the fact that its pubs have taken shape over many years, the answer, essentially, is 'no'. By and large, pubs developed in much the same ways as in the rest of the country, though with only one large city (Bristol), the South West is short on the grand late-Victorian edifices which adorn the likes of London, Birmingham, Liverpool and Manchester. On the other hand, the area is especially rich in fine rural and small town pubs, some of which are quite remarkable survivors. But first, a bit of history.

In the beginning

Most early public houses were literally just that – ordinary houses whose owners opened up a room or two to sell drink to neighbours. All you needed was somewhere to store the merchandise, somewhere to serve it and somewhere for customers to drink it. Pub keeping was a family business and, especially in the countryside, usually part-time and combined with, say, farming, carting, blacksmithing or some other trade. Nearly all these very homely pubs have gone now because such small businesses just aren't any longer an economic proposition, but the South West has some of the best remaining examples.

Top of this list has to be the Luppitt Inn, Luppitt, Devon (p.42), the epitome of the simple, unspoilt farmhouse pub, owned by the same family for more than a century and still with a few acres attached (and also with very restricted opening hours which makes visiting a challenge.) The Berkeley Arms, Purton, Gloucestershire (p.73) too has both a smallholding as part of the business and limited hours, including being closed altogether between October and Easter). Also with land attached (28 acres) is the Hunters Lodge, Priddy, Somerset (p.95). Until it was sold off in 1980, the Seymour Arms, Witham Friary, Somerset (p.97) had a whole

The Berkeley Arms, Purton is attached to a smallholding but has limited hours and is closed in winter

6

The brew house of the Blue Anchor, Helston the only pub in the UK to have brewed continuously since before the founding of CAMRA

The Haunch of Venison, Salisbury proclaims it is 'An Old English Chop House'

farm attached. Visit any of these pubs and you can get a strong flavour of the rustic simplicity of rural pubs of yesteryear.

Only six open pubs in the whole country now have no bar counter – once a common arrangement. Two of them feature in the guide – the Rose & Crown, Huish Episcopi (p.91) and Tuckers Grave, Faulkland (p.88), both in Somerset. See page xx for more information.

Something which would have been done in hundreds of pubs in the past – the brewing of beer on the premises – had dwindled by the early 1970s (when CAMRA was formed) to just four examples, one being the Blue Anchor, Helston, Cornwall (p.21). As the other three later stopped brewing, before starting again, the Blue Anchor is unique in being the only one to brew continuously. The Bruce Arms, Easton Royal, Wiltshire (p.103) did once brew its own ale and on a mantle-piece is a piece of wood from a cask impressed with the words 'Bruce Arms'.

Inns and taverns

The other types of establishment up until the early 19th century were the tavern and the inn. The former existed only in larger towns, catering for the more prosperous customer by serving wine and food. They were never common and no former taverns appear to survive in the South West although the Haunch of Venison, Salisbury (p.107) perhaps enjoys something of the atmosphere of such places (and wording on the frontage proclaims 'Old English Chop House'). In any event, it's a rare example of an urban pub that has stayed virtually unchanged for over 100 years.

Inns provided meals and accommodation for better-off travellers along with stabling for their horses. Inevitably they have been greatly modified; places which go back centuries but now retain few 'pubby' features include the George, Norton St Philip, Somerset, the New Inn, Gloucester and the George & Pilgrims, Glastonbury, Somerset – see p.76 for more details about these impressive buildings. The Luttrell Arms Hotel, Dunster, Somerset (p.84) has the most intact historic inn interior but lacks the iconic courtyard associated with such establishments.

The lounge of the Luttrell Arms, Dunster showing a very old partition wall and 17th-century ceiling

The golden age

The pub as we know it today is mostly a Victorian creation. The first part of the 19th century saw the widespread adoption of counter service and the hand-pumped beer engine, heralding the change from an essentially domestic environment into a form of shop which could handle a greater volume of trade. Just as most rural pubs once catered primarily for the agricultural labourer, vast numbers of urban pubs were fairly basic establishments for the working man. In industrial areas especially, pubs afforded welcome refreshment after a shift down the pit, in the steelworks or a day of hard labour. However, such industrialisation largely passed the South West by so pubs of this kind always were few and far between. The Lamb & Fountain, Frome, Somerset (p.90) is a 'back street boozer' like those still relatively common in other parts of the country.

Later in the century, under the influence of social reformers and the powerful Temperance lobby, a drive to improve public houses took hold. This enhanced the multi-room principle with its ability to offer a choice of 'better' rooms and thus attract a respectable clientele. Nearly all these many-roomed interiors have since been opened out but you can see a surviving partition at the Nova Scotia, Bristol (p.67). The years around 1900 proved to be the high point of pub-building and design, with grand, ornate 'palace' pubs arriving in bigger towns and cities, but also with lesser variants being built elsewhere. Sadly, the South West mostly missed this aspect of the 'golden age'. The Palace Hotel, Bristol (p.111) is the nearest to what are often (and inaccurately) termed 'gin palaces' with its impressive arcading, but even this has been much altered.

Glazed screens made their first appearance at this time but were largely a northern phenomenon. The Seymour Arms, Witham Friary, Somerset (p.97) has fine horizontally sliding windows while the Globe, Appley, Somerset (p.79) has a simpler version.

The snug at the Nova Scotia, Bristol showing a rare surviving partition

The best survivor from this era is the Kings Head, also in Bristol (p.65) with many features dating back to the middle of the 19th century, including one of the oldest bar-back fittings we know about. The late-Victorian public bar of the White Hart, Midsomer Norton, Somerset (p.93) contains much to admire. Other notable pubs from this era are the Cricketers, Bournemouth (p.52), built with a separate billiards room, and the Victoria, Oldfield Park, Bath, of 1897 (p.111).

The Kings Head, Bristol has a bar back fitting dated 1865, one of the oldest we know of

Between the Wars

The Great War brought pub-building to a full stop but it resumed quite soon afterwards. Pubs at first continued to be built on traditional lines, but before long we saw arrival of the 'improved' pub, often built for growing suburbs and busy highways. Reducing the number of pubs but improving standards in what remained had been the mission of magistrates for some years and there was now a concerted drive to broaden the appeal of pubs and reduce their dependence on alcohol sales alone. The idea was for pubs to offer a 'respectable' environment with a range of rooms and facilities that encouraged civilised behaviour and patronage by the middle classes. Having said that, although these 'improved' pubs proliferated in the rest of the country, relatively few were built in the South West and none survive with any degree of intactness.

The Corner House, Barnstaple is an excellent example of an Art Deco pub

Nonetheless, brewers responded to these developments with a fresh surge of pub-building from the mid-1920s. Art Deco was the emblematic architectural style in this period but was adopted only rarely for pubs. An excellent example is the Corner House, Barnstaple, Devon (p.34) with its typical Deco frontage and little-altered, mostly panelled interior – the curved bar counter is especially redolent of the period. Many older pubs were given makeovers in styles of the period

The inter-war panelled interior of the Old Green Tree, Bath

such as two pubs in Bath, the Old Green Tree and the Star, both refurbished by the same architect in the 1920s with plentiful panelling and a variety of small rooms. Other notable inter-war decorative schemes can be found at the Ship, Shaftesbury (p.60), and the Journey's End, Ringmore, Devon (p.46).

Post-war decline

Britain was bankrupt after the Second World War and hardly any pubs were built for a decade. When building restrictions were relaxed in 1954, new pubs began emerging again and were typified, unsurprisingly for these straightened times, by utilitarian design and low-quality materials. Layouts, though, still provided a choice of rooms and such customary features as off-sales and concert rooms. Inevitably, once the economy picked up, these cut-price reminders of post-war austerity became highly unfashionable and few intact interiors from the period remain. However, difficult to love as they may be, they are important as reminders of how and where folk drank in those increasingly distant times. Bristol has two good examples, the Hartcliffe Inn of 1958 (p.67) and the Giant Goram (p.71) of a year later. Both have two rooms and skittle alleys, the one at the Hartcliffe remarkably being open to the public bar (though a screen has been removed). The Falstaff, Plymouth (p.45), is a little later and even has a few architectural flourishes, notably the bar counter.

From the mid-1960s, pub architects started to become more adventurous and some decidedly quirky buildings, mostly now lost, took shape. Best of those remaining is the (recently statutorily listed) Centurion, Twerton, Bath (p.83), of 1965 whose striking design owes much to its hillside position. The interior takes you straight back to an era where innovation and imagination were the order of the day.

Sadly, this increased prosperity heralded a time of rapid and mostly regrettable change. The social divisions mirrored by the multi-roomed

(Top) The distinct Post-war exterior of the Centurion, Twerton, Bath and (below) the Falstaff, Plymouth (MSS)

pub were vanishing while magistrates and police favoured direct supervision of all parts of a pub from the serving area – hence the widespread removal of internal walls to the great detriment of the atmosphere and attractiveness of most traditional pubs. Many pubs throughout the South West were heavily influenced by their pub own-ing brewery in the 1960s and 1970s, some being allowed to do their own thing, whilst others had to follow the company policy (if, indeed, they had one!) on how the pub interior was presented. In later years the corporate image became all important and is discernable today, even if done in a subtle way. Some refits, such as those at the Cock & Bottle, East Morden, Dorset (p.53), and the Hunters Lodge, Priddy, Devon (p.95), displayed real care and attention but serious trashing tended to be the rule.

At the same time, a series of brewery mergers brought the majority of pubs into the ownership of one or other of the 'Big Six' national brewing conglomerates. All of these, in thrall to their corporate accountants and marketing men, inflicted huge damage on the pub heritage they inherited. Smaller brewers and many private owners shared this obsession to modernise.

There was no respite. The rise of off-licences, shops and super-markets made pub off-sales redundant (see p.112). Environmental health officers demanded changes to accommodate inside toilets and better food preparation facilities. Old bar-back fittings were hacked about to make space for more varied products like wine, spirits and refrigerated drinks. Fire officers insisted on adaptations to provide safer escape routes. Such relentless pressures resulted in a much-depleted pub heritage.

The interior of the Hunters Lodge, Priddy, which is unchanged since a refit in 1964

The aftermath

Recent years have seen a sad decline in the overall numbers of traditional pubs in this country – down from around 70,000 in 1980 to 48,500 today. To some extent, this has been offset by an increase in bars, nearly all in town and city centres, but, with some honourable exceptions, few have much merit in design terms. Some new pubs continue to be built, mostly 'family' pubs on the edges of towns, but conversions from other uses like banks and shops are much more common. The fact that, in most years, no winner can be found for the New Build category in CAMRA's annual Pub Design Awards speaks for itself.

Mentioned earlier were the particular pressures on small, rural pubs which struggle to be viable. Happily, some have successfully met this challenge by extending their building in ways which don't impact adversely on their historic core. An excellent example is the Drewe Arms, Drewsteignton, Devon (p.37), which originally comprised just the simply-appointed public bar left of the entrance. On its own, this couldn't pay its way, so further rooms, mostly for dining, have been developed elsewhere in the property – but discreetly separate. The Half Moon, Cheriton Fitzpaine, Devon (p.36) sensitively added a lounge and the George, Portland, Dorset (p.56), added a new bar in a former kitchen. The expansion of the Glasshouse Inn, May Hill, Gloucestershire (p.71) has been particularly well handled.

Public interest in our built heritage has never been higher and the existence of this very book and the popularity of others like it published by CAMRA shows that this interest extends to our pubs as well. The article on p.15 examines the threats our historic pubs face and what we can do about them.

The Glasshouse Inn, May Hill has a particularly sensitive expanded interior

CAMRA and Pub Heritage

CAMRA was founded in 1971 to save Britain's traditional beer but it soon became clear to campaigners that the best places to drink such beer, our pubs, were also under threat. In due course, CAMRA assigned equal importance to campaigning for real ale and for pubs.

The 1970s onwards saw a huge increase in the opening out of pubs and removals of fine fittings, so preservation of historic pub interiors emerged as a key campaigning issue.

After pioneering work in York in the late 1980s, a specialist Pub Preservation Group was set up, which evolved into today's Pub Heritage Group. The first step was to identify the most intact interiors surviving across the country's (then) 65,000 pubs. This massive task meant following up thousands of leads, developing criteria for inclusion, recording what was found (in words and photos) and creating a list – the National Inventory of Historic Pub Interiors (NI). This initially focused on interiors still largely unaltered since before the Second World War, though intact early post-war pubs were later admitted. A further development was to include pubs with specific features or rooms of real national importance.

The Bridge Inn, Topsham is on CAMRA's National Inventory of Historic Pub Interiors

The Horseshoe, Ebbesbourne Wake is included in *Britain's Best Real Heritage Pubs* as a 'Try Also' pub

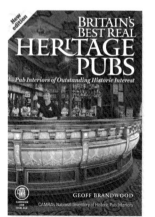

The first NI was published in 1997 and totalled 179 entries. Since then it has been continually refined and updated as new candidates were discovered and, sadly, existing entries lost. The present total stands at 278 and full descriptions can be found in our publication *Britain's Best Real Heritage Pubs*, as well as on our website (see below). 18 of these pubs are in the South West.

Regional Inventories were the next logical step. As would be expected, the criteria for inclusion are set lower than for the NI though the same principles apply, with the emphasis on the internal fabric of the pub and what is authentically old. 57 pubs of this standard can be found in the South West. The selection criteria for both National and Regional Inventories are set out on page 113.

We also acknowledge a third category – pubs that have experienced still more change but which retain historic rooms or features felt to be of 'some regional interest'. 34 such pubs are mentioned in this guide.

Inventory pubs in all three categories can be found on our website **www.pubheritage.camra.org.uk** where clicking on the Search Here facility will take you to easy-to-use drop-down menus.

Pubs in Peril

The current plight of the British pub is only too well-known. At the time of going to press, figures showed around fourteen closing each week and, in the decade ending 2018, pub numbers fell by some 11,000, representing 23% of the nation's pub stock. Many reasons can be identified for this gloomy state of affairs, including changing social habits, the effect of recent recessions, the widening differential between the prices of drinks bought at a pub and in a supermarket, the rapacious behaviour of many pub-owning companies and the smoking ban. A particular threat is the attractiveness of many pub buildings to developers. Conversion of rural pubs to houses has been all too common for many years but it's now our urban pubs which are really suffering. Many suburban pubs, for instance, occupy large plots of land, ideal for small supermarkets or similar developments, and in recent years hundreds have been lost in that way.

Such losses had been exacerbated by feeble planning laws which allowed the demolition of pubs and many changes of use without the

The public bar of the Long Acre Tavern, Bath, now a Domino's Pizza outlet.

The Waverley Arms, Weymouth, a multi-roomed 1930s pub, now a 'community hub'

need for planning permission. Strong campaigning by CAMRA and others led to these 'permitted development' rights being withdrawn in England in 2017 and the closure rate has slowed down since. We are now campaigning for similar provisions in the rest of the UK.

This combination of negative factors has posed major problems for heritage pubs, especially urban ones. Many of the latter are to be found in unfashionable, off-centre locations where they have ticked along for many years, serving the local community. As a result, their owners saw little point investing in the kinds of major change inflicted, in the pursuit of fashion, on many town or city centre pubs, so heritage was preserved, more or less by accident. Sadly, though, when the recent recessions began to bite, these pubs tended to drop the wrong side of the profit line.

Several pubs which meet the criteria for inclusion in this guide are currently closed and facing an uncertain future. They include the National Inventory-listed Red Lion at Ampney St Peter, Gloucestershire, a beautifully unspoilt one room, no-bar alehouse. After fervent campaigning from CAMRA and others, planning permission for change of use to residential was refused; the property has now been sold and we wait to learn the intentions of the new owners. The Kings Arms, Stockland, Devon and Three Crowns, Bristol have also been shut for some time while the Palace, Bristol and the Victoria, Oldfield Park, Bath were closed, temporarily we hope, at the time of going to press. See the feature on Closed Pubs (p.109) for more information.

Three pubs once being considered for the National Inventory have been wrecked or lost in recent times. The Wheatsheaf, Cheltenham was a 1933 build, originally with three rooms; although two were combined in the 1970s, it remained largely intact until 2007 when it was fully opened out and old fittings were removed. It was a similar story at the Richmond Springs (now White Rabbit), Clifton, Bristol where a series of alterations has ruined the panelled inter-war interior. The Waverley Arms, Weymouth was yet another multi-roomed Thirties pub but in this case it closed altogether and is now a 'community hub'. The Long Acre Tavern, Bath *was* included on the National Inventory as an example of an intact 1960s interior. However, English Heritage declined to list it in 2009 and it is now a Domino's Pizza outlet.

However, historic pubs in peril can be, and have been, saved and CAMRA's Pub Heritage Group will fight for every one. One tactic is to draw a threatened pub to the attention of an enlightened small pub company and several pubs elsewhere in the country have been saved in just this way. We also get pubs statutorily listed (see p.17). Where we can, we use the planning system to resist unwanted changes to heritage pubs and encourage local folk to do likewise. Most of all, we aim to generate interest in these precious survivors. Pubs are businesses and the more that people use them, the less likely are they to wither and die.

* *You can do your bit by putting this guide to active use* *

Statutory Listing

All parts of the United Kingdom have systems for protecting buildings of special architectural or historic interest. 68 of the 104 pubs in this guide are statutorily listed. The process is devised not to *prevent* change but to *manage* it effectively, working with the grain of the building, not against it.

In England, listings are made by the Secretary of State for Culture, Media and Sport, on the advice of Historic England. There are three grades:

Grade I. This highest of gradings covers just 2.5% of all listed buildings, these being those that have 'exceptional', even international, interest.

Grade II* (spoken of as 'Two Star'). Covers a further 5.5% of listed buildings which have 'outstanding interest'. Pubs in the guide which enjoy this status are the Haunch of Venison, Salisbury; the Luttrell Arms, Dunster, Somerset; the Berkeley Arms, Tewkesbury; the Drewe Arms, Drewsteignton; and the Oxenham Arms, South Zeal (the last two in Devon).

Grade II. 92% of listed buildings fall into this category; they have what is described as 'special' architectural or historic interest.

The Corner House, Barnstaple just narrowly missed a Grade II listing when under consideration as part of Historic England's Inter-War Pubs Survey in 2016

THE
SUPERIOR
PALE ALE

QUALITY SPEAKS FOR ITSELF

Cornwall

Albaston, PL18 9AJ
01822 832482
Not listed
LPA: Cornwall
🍺 🍴 (L, E)

Queens Head ☆

Basic two-bar pub refitted around 50 years ago and hardly changed since. The main bar consisted of two rooms until that time and has a shiny hardboard slanting bar front with a cream Formica top. The bar-back fitting looks to be from the 1960s with a mirrored back and a ribbed hardboard feature above. Note that bottles are stored on the

The snug has fittings from c1960

shelves on their side, not upright, and some lower shelves have given way to fridges. There is a 1960s brick fireplace painted red, some old dado panelling and leatherette seating. The off-sales hatch with ribbed hardboard on the counter front survives. On the right, a tiny snug has a three-sided counter of similar design to that in the other room plus. simple bar-back shelves, a 1960s pot-shelf above the bar and a classic pale-tiled fireplace with a gas fire. However, the licensee plans, at some stage, to reconfigure the main bar, moving the counter to the left-hand wall so best to check ahead if planning a visit.

Boscastle
High Street, PL35 0BD
01840 250204
www.napoleoninn.co.uk
Grade II listed   LPA: Cornwall
 (L, E)

Napoleon Multi-roomed, early 17th-century pub with fittings from the 1950s and not greatly changed since. The small public bar has a Delabole slate floor, slatted wooden counter, fitted seating and a stone fireplace. Similar floors and fittings are found in the other rooms – a lounge, a small room up two steps, the 'Fun Bar' in a (now old) extension and a dining room in what was a separate cottage.

The Delabole slate-floored public bar

Falmouth
1 The Moor, TR11 3QA
01326 312111
www.thesevenstarsfalmouth.com
Grade II listed
LPA: Cornwall

Seven Stars ★
This small town centre pub, built around 1800 and with a late 19th-century re-fronting, has been in the same family's hands for seven generations. For fifty of those years, until he died in 2012, the licensee was Barrington Bennetts, who was also an ordained Anglican clergyman. The public bar at the front has various late Victorian fittings along with metal stillages from the late 1940s and the rare, white marble counter-top from what was once a partitioned-off oyster bar. The walls and ceilings are covered with matchboard panelling and the gas lights at each end of the bar still work (though

Seven Stars: the little-altered public bar *(Photo by Geoff Brandwood)*

Helston
50 Coinagehall Street, TR13 8EU
01326 562821
www.spingoales.com
Grade II listed
LPA: Cornwall

not now used). A passage, with an off-sales hatch that has sliding windows and a red Formica shelf, leads to the rear smoke room with a hatch/doorway to the back of the bar. In the ceiling is a 'coffin hatch' for raising and lowering bulky items to the upper floor. The Victorian building was extended to the right in 1912 with a (now defunct) off-sales shop. Both pub and the Rev. Bennetts featured in the *Beano* comic in 2002 in which the pub was re-named 'the Reverend's Pop Shop', with a story about him selling 'pop to the whole of Beanoland' for 50 years (a cartoonist for the comic drinks here.)

Blue Anchor ☆

Thatched 18th-century pub, renowned as the only one in the UK to have continuously brewed its own beers since before CAMRA formed in 1971 (the other three then still in existence have since had non-brewing spells). From the front door, an uneven flagged passage runs through to the tiny 19th-century brew-house at the rear, with rooms off on each side. The main bar is at the front right and was once two small rooms; the counter is at least fifty years old though the top is more recent and the bar-back shelves are newer still. The small bare wall benches and the half-panelling are,

however, genuinely old. In the rear snug, with its ancient stone fireplace, the counter is a 1980s replacement. Left of the passage are three small rooms but the only old fitting is the inglenook fireplace in the first one. The brew-house is viewable on request.

One of the three small rooms left of the passage (Photo by Mark Finney)

Padstow

6–8 Lanadwell Street PL28 8AN
01841 532554
www.londoninnpadstow.co.uk
Not Listed   LPA: Cornwall
🍺 🍴 (L, E)

London Inn ☆

Although the small front bar was once divided into two small rooms (hence 'Bar' and 'Private Bar' on the windows), it retains its Victorian counter, painted a deep red colour, and old bar-back shelves – a real rarity in Cornwall. Tongue-and-grooved wall-panelling, old wall-bench seating, a stone fireplace and a square panelled ceiling complete the picture. Beyond the partitioning with lattice leaded windows is the bar counter of the private bar and at the rear is a hatch/doorway which could once have been an off-sales. Through a wide doorway to the right is another small room with half-height panelling, a stone/slate fireplace and more aged wall benches. The small restaurant to the rear right occupies a room brought into use not long ago.

The servery in the public bar

Penzance
46 Chapel Street, TR18 4AF
01736 363448
www.thebenbow.com
Grade II Listed
LPA: Cornwall
  (L, E)

Entrance to the Great Cabin

Admiral Benbow ★

18th-century pub with an extraordinary interior, the creation of which was begun in the late 1950s by former owner and diver Roland Morris. The Great Cabin is a spectacular themed room utilising fittings from wrecked ships to re-create the aft cabin of a privateer, though it now contains some later 'standard' items like bench tables and seating. Please note, though, that this room is laid out as a restaurant and used as such in the summer season; in winter it is only open for occasional functions, but the staff will generally be happy to let you view. Upstairs is the Wreck Room, again only used in the summer, and otherwise acting as a store room. Artefacts and trinkets are not set out in any order or theme. The public bar, front right, has a sloping bar counter and a copper top; the bar-back is a mix of old and new shelves. Also in this room are small seating bays on stone bases, round tables with copper tops and a panelled ceiling. To the left are more seating areas, a brick fireplace with carved mantelpiece (another shipwreck item) and nautical artefacts in abundance.

The Old and the Odd

Some oldies

The UK is stuffed with pubs claiming to be its oldest and the South West's main culprit is the former Royalist Hotel, now Porch House, in Stow-on-the-Wold, Gloucestershire. The pub's website claims it was founded in AD949 as a hospice to shelter lepers. Historic England say the building is possibly 16th century, remodelled in the 17th century (it has a 1615 date-stone) but a pub is not recorded here until the 18th century. The myths around the building seem to originate from a lecture of 1861 by a local vicar based on some very dodgy speculations.

The oldest item in a South West pub must be the 5,000 year old monolith in the Oxenham Arms, South Zeal, Devon (p.47), while the bar-back at the Kings Head, Bristol

(p.65), dated 1865, is the second-oldest we are aware of, narrowly younger than that at the Victoria, Bayswater W2 (1864).

At the time of writing, the oldest licensee was Mary Wright at the Luppitt Inn, Luppitt, Devon (98) with Freda 'Mother' Searle of the Lamb & Fountain, Frome, Somerset, not far behind at 96. Historically, the region's longest-serving landlady was Mabel Mudge

of the Drewe Arms, Drewsteignton, Devon, who retired in 1994, aged 99, having been in charge since 1919.

Finally, we must mention the amazing Valiant Soldier in Buckfastleigh, Devon. Having been in the same family for 30 years, it closed in 1968 – but the landlady lived there for a further 30 years, leaving the bar area untouched. When she moved to a nursing home, the Council bought the building and reopened it as a museum in 2000. Everything is as it was when time was last called, with artefacts and

The 5,000 year old Monolith at the Oxenham Arms, South Zeal

The Valient Soldier, Buckfastleigh

living accommodation dating back to the 1940s and 1950s. As a time capsule it is, therefore, unique. It is open from Easter to the end of October, Monday to Saturday (and Bank Holiday Sundays) from 12.30pm to 4.30pm. Entrance price covers both the Valiant Soldier and Buckfastleigh Museum – more at **www.valiantsoldier.org.uk** (no drinks on sale!)

Some oddities

In any survey of pubs, you'll come across some which just don't 'fit' as part of a historical narrative because they are essentially quirky one-offs.

The Admiral Benbow, Penzance (p.23), meets the criteria for this guide and this fascinating pub-cum-maritime museum is a must see when in the area and a jolly nice place for a pint to boot.

Not featured here but well worth a visit is the totally bonkers Highwayman Inn at Sourton, Devon. From 1959 onwards, the owner set about 'improving' the pub in a highly eccentric manner, starting by positioning the old Launceston to Taunton mail-coach as the entrance porch. The dimly-lit interior is home to all manner of weirdness – a make-believe sailing galleon, a 'pixies' haunt', a grotto of stuffed animals (mostly local road-kill) and so on. The mix of the gory and the twee isn't for everyone but you can't say it isn't different.

An early example (also not in this book) is the Pack of Cards, Combe Martin, Devon, reputedly built as a private house in 1690 after a spectacular gambling win. The number of windows, doors, chimneys etc. reflected the component features of a pack of cards e.g. four storeys, 13 rooms, 52 windows. The shape was that of a house built of cards.

The Wreck Room at the Admiral Benbow, Penzance, one of the oddest pub interiors in the country

Philleigh, TR2 5NB
01872 580254
www.roselandinn.co.uk
Not listed
LPA: Cornwall
🍺 🍴 (L, E)

The locals' bar

Roseland ☆

Locals say that the interior here has changed little since the 1950s. The main bar is to the left of the central flagstone passage and has a counter in 'publican's rustic' style, an old brick fireplace and a mix of old and new panelling. At the back is a tiny locals bar, the counter being an extension of the bar-back fitting. The dining room, far right, came into public use only recently. Note that the staff serve from a floor level about a foot below that of the bar.

Port Isaac
13 Fore Street, PL29 3RB
01208 880336
www.thegoldenlionportisaac.
co.uk
Grade II listed
LPA: Cornwall
🍺 🍴 (L, E)

Golden Lion ☆

Early 18th-century pub near the harbour end of the steep narrow main street. A sizeable entrance hall with half-height panelling has a former off-sales hatch and a corner seat for drinkers. The small bare-boarded bar on the left has an old counter, Victorian tiled, cast-iron and wood surround fireplace, old dado panelling and wall-bench seating, but the bar-back is recent. In the bar on the right, also bare-boarded, are a post-war counter, modern bar-back, old fireplace, window bench and corner settle. The patio doors are a later insertion. A wide opening gives into a third room, formerly in domestic use, with an old range fireplace. Upstairs, two rooms have been merged to form the dining room.

The small left-hand bar in the Golden Lion

Portscatho

The Square, TR2 5HW
01872 580321
www.plumeoffeathers-roseland.com
Not listed   LPA: Cornwall
🍺 🍎   🍴 (L, E)

below Painted glass window; the naïve painting on the cellar door

Plume of Feathers Included here for the Old Bar at the rear, from where you can view both the old servery and the split door of the Cellar Bar with its painted glass windows above and naive painting below. The servery itself has a flagstone floor; in the right corner is an old bar-back with a pewter top to the middle part, old mirrors and brass-edged shelves held up by plain columns. Also in this area are a beam and plank ceiling, three small cupboards and a window seat – note the old Worthington illuminated sign on the bar-back. The Cellar Bar is to the left of the main room (which has modern fittings).

The old bar back

St Agnes

10 Vicarage Road, TR5 0TJ
01872 552310
Grade II listed
LPA: Cornwall

🍺 🍴 (L, E; not Mon, Tue)

The main bar is little-altered since the 1940s

Railway Inn ☆

Although refitted in the late 1940s, the original plan of four small rooms plus off-sales remains discernible at this 19th-century stone-built pub. A panelled passage leads from the front door to the former off-sales hatch, to the left of which is a small old counter. Front left, the small 'Commercial Room' has an inter-war fireplace and old wall cupboards; the original door is the now half-height one in the passage, the currently used opening coming later. Another small room, front right, was once a ladies' parlour and has old panelling and another wall cupboard. A wide gap leads into the main bar with a counter that is older than it looks (in features in a photo taken in the late 1940s), plus panelled walls and a brick fireplace. A cottage on the left was incorporated into the pub, adding two more rooms.

St Just-in-Penwith

1 Fore Street, TR19 7LL
01736 788767
www.thestarinn-stjust.co.uk
Grade II listed   LPA: Cornwall

🍺

Penlee lifeboat disaster remembrance

Star Inn ☆

From the front door of this 18th-century granite building, a passage runs to the back via an inner door with Victorian glasswork (note the rare bitumen floor here and in the main bar). The public bar on the left was extended in the late 1950s to incorporate the former snug; the counter is from the same period but the mirrored bar-back long pre-dates it. There is old panelling in the main bar but the rustic brick fireplace is new; a candle is always lit during opening hours in remembrance of the Penlee lifeboat disaster of 1981 in which sixteen people died, including eight volunteer lifeboatmen. Right of the passage, through a door with a number 2 plus the barest outline of the designation 'Commercial Room', two rooms were amalgamated in recent times – the rear part has a superb granite fireplace with integral bread oven.

The Star Inn public bar
last changed in the 1950s

St Teath

The Square, PL30 3JX
01208 850281
Not listed
LPA: Cornwall
 (L, E)

White Hart Multi-roomed pub largely rebuilt in 1844 and with an especially good public bar – Delabole slate floor, rare Art Deco fireplace, very old high-backed settle and chunky inter-war bar counter (with no bar-back fitting). Several of the other rooms were brought into use or altered quite recently. The small room at the front right has fixed seating and half-timbering from the 1960s while the tiny Cellar Bar behind the servery was created in the 1950s and is served by a hatch.

The public bar with a rare Art Deco fireplace

Stratton

Fore Street, EX23 9DA
01288 352038
www.treeinn.co.uk
Grade II listed
LPA: Cornwall

 (L, E)

Tree Inn ☆

16th-century coaching inn, where two rooms retain fittings from the 1950s. The Beville Bar, rear right, has an old slate floor and a draught screen/high-backed settle with glazed panels above. The lapped-wood counter was created in the 1950s from coffin sides from a local undertaker! Photos taken around 1960 show the old dresser which forms the bar-back fitting and which sits in an old fireplace. To the left of the coaching arch, the heavily-beamed dining room also has a (copper-topped) counter from the 1950s. The public bar, once probably two rooms, has seen several recent changes though the beams and some of the panelling are old. The Cornish giant, Anthony Payne, is said to have been born here around 1612; he grew to 7ft 4ins tall and weighed 32 stones.

The Beville Bar with its high-backed settle

Tregadillet, PL15 7 EU

01566 772051
www.theeliotarms.co.uk
Not listed
LPA: Cornwall

 (L, E)

The left-hand bar

Eliot Arms (Square & Compass) Attractive country hotel with five separate rooms. The original pub consisted of the small bars front and rear with extra rooms being added over the years. Notable features include the old curved bar counter at the rear right, the Delabole slate floors from the nearby quarry (reputedly the largest man-made hole in Britain) and antique high-backed settles.

Tywardreath

Fore Street, PL24 2QP
01726 813901
www.staustellbrewery.co.uk/
pub/tywardreath/new-inn
Grade II listed   LPA: Cornwall
🍺 🍴(L, E) 🛏

New Inn ☆

Although the pub claims a build date of 1752, the listing description puts this as '19th-century'. The portico on the front was supposedly moved from the 'town hall' next door in 1932. Inside, the public bar on the left is little changed. The panelled counter has, on top, a slotted brass plate for tokens issued by the local copper mine owner. Draught Bass is sold from casks stillaged behind the bar – apparently a covenant requirement from the sale to St Austell in 1932. The bar-back shelves

and mirrors are recent but the panelling on both the walls and above the servery is old as are the benches. A side door, first right, leads to the small smoking room, then a door sporting the number 4 takes you to a bare-boarded passageway at the end of which are the remains of the former off-sales. Rear right is the music room, with the figure 2 on the door, and rear left a bistro brought into use quite recently.

Slots on the counter top for the copper mine tokens

The unchanged public bar

31

Table Service

In some old pubs, you will find bell-pushes dotted round a room. Hardly any of these still work but they are a reminder of a largely forgotten practice – table service. The bells connected to a box in, or visible from, the servery where a bell would ring and an indicator wobble to show where a customer was in need of a drink. A member of the servery staff or a dedicated waiter would go and take the order, then deliver it. Needless to say, prices in these rooms were a touch higher than in the public bar and a copper or two by way of a tip to the server was customary. The system worked very efficiently in busy pubs as the waiting staff usually went to a dedicated area of the counter from which other customers were excluded so that they didn't have to fight their way through a crowd of stand-up drinkers.

Good examples of (now-defunct) bell-pushes can be seen in the delightful Tramcar Bar at the Kings Head, Bristol (p.65) and in the tap room at Tucker's Grave,

Bell-push in the Tap Room at the Tucker's Grave, Faukland

The annunciator box at the Star, Bath

Faulkland, Somerset (p.88). As for bell-boxes, examples exist behind the serveries at both the Star, Bath (p.81) and the Ship, Shaftesbury (p.60).

In olden days, when pubs were beer-houses, your drinks would be brought to you from the cellar by

The annunciator box at the Ship Inn, Shaftesbury

the licensee (and sometimes on a tray). Amazingly, this still happens at the very traditionally-run Bridge Inn, Topsham, Devon (p.48).

Elsewhere in the country, the traditional form of table service survives in a handful of pubs. However, as with the off-licence (see p.112), the practice is making a come-back and, as with off-sales, the J D Wetherspoon chain is responsible. You can now order drinks and food from the comfort of your seat, albeit using an app on your phone rather than pushing a bell – and it won't cost you a penny more.

Bell pushes in the Tramcar Bar at the Kings Head, Bristol

Beer brought from the cellar to the customer at the Bridge, Topsham

Devon

Abbotskerswell
Totnes Road (A381), TQ12 6DF
01803 812411
www.twomileoakinn.co.uk
Grade II listed
LPA: Teignbridge
 (L, E)

Two Mile Oak 17th-century former farmhouse with later extensions. An attractive porch with bare benches each side leads to a tiny internal lobby with inter-war leaded panels in a screen and a split door which may once have accessed an off-sales. Within the multi-roomed interior, the public bar has old dado panelling, wall benches and unusual seating round the fireplace. Elsewhere, many of the fittings are quite recent but some old features survive.

The right-hand rooms (MSS)

Barnstaple

108 Boutport Street, EX31 1SY
01271 343528
Not listed
LPA: North Devon

The barely-altered 1935 public bar

Corner House ★

Re-built in 1935 with an Art Deco curved frontage (see p. 9) and little altered since – a remarkable survivor, particularly given its town-centre location. The main bar was originally two small rooms which accounts for its current L-shape. The walls sport fielded panelling to three-quarter height plus a curved bar counter with black Formica top, a two-sided bar-back fitting and a 1930s inglenook-style fireplace. The original off-sales is now used for storage. On the right, the snug (now called 'Garlands') has more fielded panelling – the bar counter appears to be a replacement from around 1960. The gents are unaltered. A skittle alley occupies a single-storey extension; it has the original ball-run topped by benching on the right side with further seating on the left.

Berrynarbour

Pit Hill, EX34 9SG
01271 882465
Not listed
LPA: North Devon
 (L, E)

Ye Olde Globe Inn ☆

An excellent example of how to expand a village pub and retain its character. Originally three cottages, it now consists of six rooms. The Kitchen bar, front right, is one of the two original public rooms and is unchanged in years. It has fixed settle-like seating around the fireplace – one acting as a draught protector by the front door – an ancient screed floor, old seating attached to the dado and an old bench. The exterior-style windows indicate this was the original extent of the

The Kitchen bar

building. Through a doorway is the Village Bar, added around 1960, hence the 'half-timbering' on the walls redolent of the period. The pool room beyond is in a yet later extension as is the function room. Front centre is the original second public room with another screed floor, settles, barrel tables and stools. It was extended back around 1960 when the bar counter was added (it has a modern top). Behind the bar are shelving and furniture/fittings from the same period. Note the old glass display case containing chocolates etc. On the front left, a former domestic area is now a dining room.

Chagford
High Street, TQ13 8AJ
01647 433485
www.theglobeinnchagford.co.uk
Grade II listed LPA: West Devon
🍺 🍴(L, E)

Globe The public bar at this mid-19th-century inn retains its Victorian counter, a bar-back with mirrors and slender pillars thought to date from the 1930s, old panelling around the walls with benches attached and a large stone fireplace with wood surround. The lounge on the right was two rooms until the 1970s whilst a lovely off-sales was removed in 2004.

The public bar with its Victorian counter

Cheriton Fitzpaine
Lag Hill, EX17 4JW
01363 866219
Grade II listed
LPA: Mid Devon
🍺 🍴 (L, E)

Half Moon Inn ☆

Built as a house in 1630, this rendered pub was much altered in the 19th and 20th centuries. Front left, two rooms have been combined into one; the bar counter is Victorian but the bar-back shelves are from the 1960s. The hatch to the left of the counter may have been the off-sales. Elsewhere are a 1950s brick fireplace, old settle, old dado wall panelling and a fine set of barrels hanging from a beam. A rare and splendid part-glazed partition separates this room from the lounge, service to which is from a hatch with a still-intact window in the screen. This small room has old dado panelling, a 1960s stone fireplace and an alcove converted from a cupboard. The ladies' toilets were once a snug hence the dado panelling. 1986 saw the addition of a big extension containing a bar and a skittle alley. The pub has been in the same family since 1945 who, until around 2000, also ran a service garage from the back of the building.

The rare partition between the lounge and the public bar

Culmstock (on B3391) EX15 3JJ
01884 799823
www.theculmvalleyinn.co.uk
Not listed   LPA: Mid Devon
🍺 🍴 (L, E)

Culm Valley Inn The best area here is the small, bare-boarded public bar with old counter, partly-old servery, 1930s fireplace and modern settle. It has been opened up to the small room on the right which has an old fireplace plus a curious tree-trunk table. Two further rooms contain little of heritage interest apart from more fireplaces.

The left-hand public bar (MSS)

Drewsteignton

The Square, EX6 6QN
01647 281224
www.drewearms.com
Grade II* listed
LPA: West Devon
🗑 🍴 (L, E)

Drewe Arms ★

Idyllically situated on the village's picture-postcard square, this pub has evolved within a row of cottages. The foremost space is the simply-appointed public bar on the left with the ground-floor 'cellar' behind. The former has plain seating round the walls and service through a hatch to the cellar where the casks are stillaged. The right-hand room has long been a dining area. Further right is another room in restaurant use; the Rayburn stove shows this was once a kitchen area. The Drewe Arms is a legend in the annals of historic rural pubs. For 75 years, it was kept by Mabel Mudge who, when she retired aged 99 in 1994, was thought to have been England's oldest licensee. Until her retirement, the pub was part of a working farm. Originally the Druid Arms, the pub name changed in the 1920s at the instigation of Julius Drewe, tea merchant and founder of the Home & Colonial grocery stores, who built the amazing Edwin Lutyens-designed Castle Drogo nearby. In the public bar note the delightful framed poetic homage to those who fought in the Great War and the pleasure afforded to the survivors by the pub you are enjoying more than 100 years on.

The simply-appointed public bar

Church House Inns

Although they can be found elsewhere in the region (and the country), Devon is especially rich in the type of pub known as Church House Inns.

The history of these pubs begins in the 15th century when many churches were used not just for worship but for retail and social activities as well. The church authorities decided that the latter must move elsewhere and, usually, houses adjacent to the church were bought or, if already church-owned, reclassified and used for non-ecclesiastical purposes. Originally, most would have been multi-functional, serving as parish hall and general meeting place as well as a church-controlled ale house but, over time, some were turned into poor houses and others settled down as public houses. They usually had a large fireplace for warming and cooking and a brewhouse with a well. In many cases, the buildings began life as cottages for the masons engaged in building the church and this is certainly the case with the Church House Inn, Rattery and the Duke of York, Iddesleigh.

Sadly, most of these pubs, whilst occupying very old buildings, have been much changed internally and sport modern bar fittings. Exceptions, listed and described in this book, are the aforementioned Duke of York (p.40), the Church House Inn,

Stoke Gabriel (p.47) and the Royal Oak, Meavy (p.43). However, many of the others retain features of considerable historic interest.

The Church House Inn, Harberton has a particularly impressive oak partition to the right of the bar counter. The Grade II* listing description refers to it as a 'plank and muntin screen' – 'muntin' is a vertical member in timber panelling separating two panels so what you have here are large oak beams as a frame with oak panelling in between. There was once another screen on the left, beyond which were private quarters. The fittings here are all recent, the bar counter and bar-back apparently imported from a bank in 1985.

Another ancient partition can be found at the Church House Inn, Rattery, also Grade II* listed, but is now largely a number of standing timbers with a wide but old arch to a small area with Formica panels on the dado. Most of the fixtures and fittings date from the 1930s or 1970s.

At Torbryan, the original public rooms in the Old Church House Inn are the present public bar, the small room in the middle and the lounge – but there were significant alterations 30 years ago. A very old and impressive stud and panel screen, incorporating a bench and stone fireplace, does though survive. The inglenook fireplace in the lounge is also rather splendid and this building, too, is listed Grade II*

The Church House Inn, Stoke Gabriel (MSS)

The public bar at the Haunch of Venison, Salisbury, which was originally a church house

The much opened-out Church House Inn, Churchstow features a heavily-beamed main bar, an old, long, bar counter and three attractive stone fireplaces. In Holne, the Church House Inn has a medieval dark oak screen separating the middle bar from the Kingsley Room. (Charles Kingsley was born in the nearby vicarage.) The Church House Inn, Stokeinteignhead and Bishop Lacy, Chudleigh complete the list of those we know about in Devon. The Haunch of Venison, Salisbury, Wiltshire (p.107) is believed to have originated as the church house for St Thomas's, situated just behind the pub.

The oak partition at the Church House Inn, Harberton (MSS)

Horsebridge, PL19 8PJ
01822 870214
www.royalinn.co.uk
Grade II listed
LPA West Devon
🍺 🍴 (L, E)

The stone-flagged public bar

Royal Inn ☆

An early 19th-century building with pointed Gothic windows characteristic of the time. The nearby bridge, built in 1437, was the lowest on the Tamar until the one at Gunnislake was constructed. A seal leaded into the granite step as you enter the porch was reputedly given by Charles I for "services rendered". The public bar is the original part of the pub and has slate-flagged floors and painted rubblestone walls. The bar counter used to face you as you entered but a major remodelling in the 1950s saw it shifted to the side to create an island arrangement serving both bars – it's an excellent example of so-called "publican's rustic". The fireplace is basically original but had a lintel added during the changes. The lounge was created in the refit from former living quarters. The bar counter on this side is a rather ugly slatted and grooved affair and the fireplace, stonework and benching are all typical of the period. A restaurant beyond occupies a later extension but doesn't impinge.

Iddesleigh
(On B3217) EX19 8BG
01837 810253
www.dukeofyorkdevon.co.uk
Grade II listed
LPA West Devon
🍺 🍴 (L, E) 🛏

Duke of York ☆

Thatched mid-17th-century inn, constructed as a row of four cottages into which the pub has expanded over the years. The oldest part is what is now the dining room. The public bar is especially characterful – it has a stone fireplace with bread oven, half-height panelling, bench seating, simple bar-back shelves and, thanks to intentional non-decoration for 60 years, a wonderful nicotine colour scheme on the ceiling and some walls. A later expansion to an area on the right does not detract. Other rooms also sport superb large fireplaces.

The public bar with casks on stillage (MSS)

Ilfracombe
Hillsborough Road, EX34 9PG
01271 864450
www.thethatchedinn.pub
Grade II listed
LPA: North Devon
🍺 🍴 (L, E)

Thatched Inn ☆

Despite appearances, a pub has only occupied the premises since 1964. On the ground floor, the Manor Bar was once two rooms and is now divided by a back-to-back fireplace. The very old panelling pre-dates the pub use but the copper-topped counter and shelves are typical 1960s work, as is the copper hood on the fireplace. Classic 1960s signage leads you upstairs to the Tower Bar which has old loose furniture but the small bar counter was removed in 2008. A separate thatched building to the right houses the gents', kitchen and cellar. It's claimed that the stone tower building in front, which incorporates a wishing well, dates from 1271, although this seems rather unlikely.

The Manor Bar with its copper bar counter top (MSS)

Luppitt, EX14 4RT
01404 891613
Not listed
LPA: East Devon

Luppitt Inn ★

A rare example of a simple, unspoilt farmhouse pub of the type that would have been common a couple of generations ago, but is now virtually extinct. It has been in the same family ownership for over a century and still has a few acres attached for rearing sheep. The building itself is a modest, two-storey Victorian affair, built of local stone. The entrance is in the yard and the pub part occupies two rooms with a red quarry-tiled hallway between them. The room in regular use, on the right, is tiny and has nothing at all sophisticated about it – a simple servery with a few shelves and beer drawn direct from a polypin behind the counter. The left-hand room was used for meetings and overspill from the main bar but is now largely disused. Outside gents' and ladies' loos. At the time of writing, only open Thursday and Saturday evenings from 8pm.

The simple public bar of this farmhouse pub

Lydford, EX20 4BH
01822 820241
www.castleinnlydford.co.uk
Not listed   LPA: West Devon
🍺 🍴 (L, E)

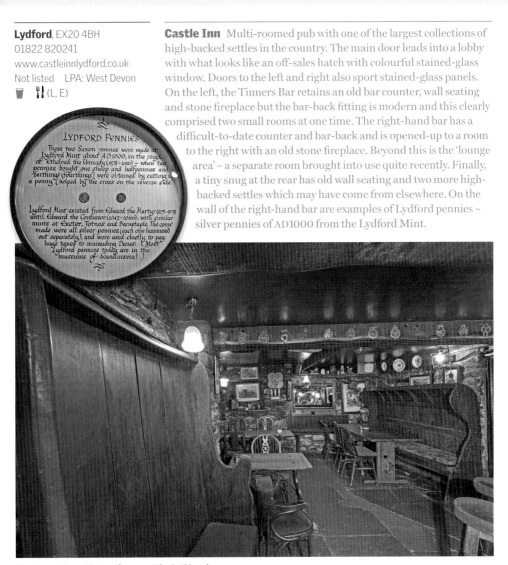

LYDFORD PENNIES
These two Saxon pennies were made at Lydford Mint about AD 1000, in the reign of Ethelred the Unready (978-1016) – when two pennies bought one sheep and halfpennies and farthings (fourthings) were obtained by cutting up a penny (helped by the cross on the reverse side).

Lydford Mint existed from Edward the Martyr (975-979) until Edward the Confessor (1042-1066), with similar mints at Exeter, Totnes and Barnstaple. The coins made were all silver pennies (each one hammered out separately), and were used chiefly to pay huge taxes to marauding Danes. (Most Lydford pennies today are in the museums of Scandinavia!)

Castle Inn Multi-roomed pub with one of the largest collections of high-backed settles in the country. The main door leads into a lobby with what looks like an off-sales hatch with colourful stained-glass window. Doors to the left and right also sport stained-glass panels. On the left, the Tinners Bar retains an old bar counter, wall seating and stone fireplace but the bar-back fitting is modern and this clearly comprised two small rooms at one time. The right-hand bar has a difficult-to-date counter and bar-back and is opened-up to a room to the right with an old stone fireplace. Beyond this is the 'lounge area' – a separate room brought into use quite recently. Finally, a tiny snug at the rear has old wall seating and two more high-backed settles which may have come from elsewhere. On the wall of the right-hand bar are examples of Lydford pennies – silver pennies of AD 1000 from the Lydford Mint.

The Tinners Bar with two of many settles in this pub

Meavy, PL20 6PJ
01822 852944
www.royaloakinn.org.uk
Grade II listed
LPA: West Devon
🍺 🍎 🍴 (L, E)

Royal Oak A 15th-century former church house inn, now owned by Burator Parish Council – only a handful of pubs nationwide are parish council-owned. There are two bars either side of a flagstoned passage. The left-hand room has massive roof beams and a counter with horizontal boarding suggestive of an inter-war date. The same design features in the other bar which also has a stone-flagged floor, vast inglenook fireplace and some fixed seating, with a shaped bench-end by the doorway.

Royal Oak: the left-hand bar of this
Parish Council-owned pub (MSS)

Newton Abbot

99 East Street, TQ12 2LD

01626 354221

Grade II listed

LPA: Teignbridge

A wide range of cider but no beer

Ye Olde Cider Bar One of only four cider houses left in the UK. Cider was once stillaged in the heart of the pub in giant hogsheads and customers wanting off-sales would use the little hatch now concealed behind doors right of the entrance. A counter was first installed in 1962 and the current layout dates from 1984 when the counter, with its curious bulging barrel-shaped slats, was moved to the present position.

Paignton

42 Elmbank Road, TQ4 5NG

01803 558322

Not listed

LPA: Torbay

Devonport Arms ☆

Victorian building revamped in the early 1930s and retaining four rooms and a good number of old fittings. The original bar counter serves three rooms and fragments of the old bar-back exist. A tiled fireplace, herringbone parquet floor in the public bar, some etched windows and both sets of gents urinals are also from the 1930s. The smallest room occupies the former jug and bottle which is tapered to fit the site.

Devonport Arms: the main bar (MSS)

Plymouth
75 Clittaford Road,
Southway, PL6 6DT
07944 610763
www.falstaffplymouth.co.uk
Not listed   LPA: Plymouth

Falstaff ☆

1960s-built estate pub which, unlike most interiors from that era, has suffered little change. It's not conventionally attractive, at least to some eyes, but is a rare reminder of a once-common decorative style. In the cavernous public bar, the counter is a real period piece – stone panels with copper strips on the front below a chunky wooden top. The bar-back is simple but intact and elsewhere are a raised balustraded section with bench seating on two sides, a darts area with pillared partitions (one of which has been reduced to half height) and a lino-tiled pool area at the far end. The L-shaped lounge also has a counter redolent of its period with the panels also appearing above the bar and carried on around the corner, plus another simple bar-back (some shelves removed) and more balustrades. A hatch for food service is currently out of use.

The 1960s bar counter (MSS)

Plymouth

7 Stopford Place,
Devonport, PL1 4QT
01752 561330
Not listed
LPA: Plymouth
🍺 🍴 (L, E)

Lounge The front section here retains a number of attractive fittings from a refit in the 1930s, notably plentiful fielded panelling, a sloping panelled counter, the bar-back and fireplace. Two doors indicate this was once two rooms. Up steps, the lounge area has seen significant alterations since the war, including loss of a snug; the fittings are also generally quite recent. Behind the rear servery is a cabinet with three large doors, indicating this was used to store casks of beer until quite recently.

The inter-war panelled interior (MSS)

Kingsbridge

Ringmore, TQ7 4HL
01548 810205
www.thejourneysendinn.co.uk
Grade II listed · LPA: South Hams
🍺 🍴 (L, E)

Journey's End Inn ☆

A fascinating pub, though by no means as old as the 'A.D. 1300' painted outside would have us believe; Historic England date it as 18th and 19th century. It was created out of four cottages with extensions between the wars and again in the 1980s. The entrance corridor (modern panelling) leads to the dining room on the right and on the left an intimate small snug with '2' over the doorway; this has stable-door service, part stone-flagged flooring and a little old panelling. Beyond, the main bar is an inter-war creation with panelling and a fireplace typical of the time plus a wide hatch to the servery where casks are stillaged.

The inter-war main bar

South Zeal, EX20 2JT
01837 840244
www.theoxenhamarms.com
Grade II* listed
LPA: West Devon
 (L, E)

Oxenham Arms Hotel ☆

Delightful two-storey 16th or early 17th-century granite inn with a grand stone porch. A stone passageway runs to the reception at the rear with, halfway along, a hatch in an old door. The beamed bar on the left was last altered in the 1960s when the area left of the granite fireplace was opened out. The solid wood counter and wall seating date from the inter-war period and casks are stillaged behind the bar. In the small lounge behind the servery a large monolith/megalith set into the wall is believed to be 5,000 years old. The mantel-piece in the dining room at the rear is supported on a huge upright splinter of granite. Another impressive stone fireplace, with a massive stone lintel, resides in the dining room front right (originally the residents' lounge).

The public bar

Stockland
Honiton Road, EX14 9BS

Kings Arms ☆

Closed at the time of writing – *see* Closed Pubs (p.109)

Stoke Gabriel
Church Walk, TQ9 6SD
01803 782384
Grade II listed LPA: South Hams
(L, E)

Church House Inn The least-altered example of the many church house inns in Devon. The last major change was in the 1960s when a large hole was cut in the public bar panelling to remove a hatch and create a bar counter. The lounge has an oak partition wall, typical of these pubs. See more about church house inns on p.38–9.

The small public bar (MSS)

Teignmouth

20 Teign Street, TQ14 8EG

01626 772684

Grade II listed

LPA: Teignbridge

The left-hand lounge (MSS)

Teign Brewery Inn ☆

Thousands of small back-street boozers once looked like this stuccoed, two-storey Victorian town pub. Architecture, layout and fittings are all simple but surprisingly complete. The plan comprises a central entrance leading to an off-sales compartment, with a separate bar either side and a further one rear right. The counters have plain vertical boarding and the bar-back fittings seem mostly modern. There is plain dado panelling and a variety of old and modern seating.

Topsham

Bridge Hill, EX3 0QQ

01392 873862

www.cheffers.co.uk/bridge.html

Grade II listed

LPA: Exeter

  (L)

Please remember this little parlour is **not** a public area and is regarded as our family sitting room.

Bridge Inn ★

Run by the same family since 1897, this glorious pub is one of the most unspoilt in the country and, in 1998, was even accorded the only official visit to a pub by Her Majesty The Queen. The entrance, on the side, leads to a panelled corridor, on the left of which is the tap room, quite plainly appointed and with some fixed seating. A little further on, you will see a bulge to the right. This is the back of an old settle, glazed at the top, in what is called the snug (by customers) or the lounge (by the owners). It features a large stone fireplace, some fixed bench seating and a grandfather clock dating from 1726. On the right is a hatch to a parlour through which drinks are fetched from the ground-floor cellar. Known as the 'Inner Sanctum', this parlour area is a private space in which customers may be *invited* to sit – only two other pubs in the country have similar rooms where customers can sit in a space behind what is a working serving area (the Arden Arms, Stockport and Ye Horns, Goosnargh, Lancashire). At the rear, the malt-house room is only used for functions or as an overflow when the pub is busy. The bar counter here was installed in the mid-1960s but the brick fireplace is inter-war and one of the old hop shoots survives.

The 'Inner Sanctum' where you need an invite to sit

Between the cellar and the malt-house is a brick-built furnace that provided hot air for hop-drying and malting operations. At quiet times, the bar staff will happily open it up for you to take a peek.

Widecombe-in-the-Moor

TQ13 7TF   01364 621327

www.rugglestoneinn.co.uk

Grade II listed

LPA: Teignbridge

🍺 🍴(L,E)

Rugglestone Inn ☆

A pub since 1832, and named after a local logan stone (a rocking stone), the Rugglestone remained unspoilt until 1993 but retains much of interest. The original layout comprised a passageway from the front door to a hatch from where you ordered your drink (and where you can still stand to get served) plus the small tap room on the front right; the present public bar, front left, was a meeting room and not in regular use. A counter was installed there in 1993 by knocking a hole in the wall to the side of the cellar. Beer is still served from casks on an old stillage. The tap room has a concrete-screeded floor, old window shutters and a 1930s fireplace. Note the illustrations of Widecombe Fair on the wall. The small rear-right room, formerly the landlady's parlour, came into pub use in the late 1990s.

The door to the cellar where you can still be served

West Country or 'Western' Skittles

In many areas, a particular pub game is both popular and rarely found elsewhere – for instance Bagatelle (Chester), Corks (South Wales valleys) and Toad in the Hole (East Sussex). In the South West, the equivalent game is West Country Skittles.

The game usually involves nine pins and three balls but beyond that there are many variations in rules, technique, scoring systems and the number of players in a team. No two alleys are the same and even the size and weights of the balls and pins can vary. Balls can be made from rubber or resin, which tend to be near perfect spheres or rough hewn from wood when any sense of uniformity is abandoned. Players deliver three balls and try to knock over as many skittles as possible. The technique usually involves an underarm bowl although a tournament was once witnessed in Dorset where players hurled the balls double-handed whilst diving forward from a squatting position!

Hartcliffe Inn, Hartcliffe, Bristol (MSS)

Most alleys are at least 24 feet long (but can exceed 30 feet in some pubs) and around 6 feet wide. The skittles tend to be cigar shaped and around 4.5 inches at their widest. In some variations there is a larger kingpin and the player's score is not counted unless this skittle is knocked over. The nine skittles are arranged in a square at the end of an alley so that the sides of the square are diagonal to the edges of the alley. Unlike in ten-pin bowling, the spacing of the skittles is wider than the ball diameter which somewhat frustratingly will allow what looks like a well-delivered ball to pass through the pins without contacting any of them.

Each skittle knocked down scores one point and if all nine are toppled (a sticker), and the player still has some of their three throws left, they are reset. This means the maximum score in a player's turn would be 27. Normally the match will be played over a series of 'legs' (where each player has a turn delivering 3 balls) and the team with the most points at the end are the winners.

Sadly, just like traditional pubs, this integral part of the region's cultural heritage is under threat.

Corner House, Barnstaple

An alley takes up a lot of space that can be used for a more lucrative restaurant in the popular tourist areas and changes of use are happening. If you want to try or witness West Country Skittles the pubs featured in this book with alleys are:

Blue Anchor, Helston, Cornwall
Corner House, Barnstaple, Devon
Ye Olde Globe Inn, Berrynarbour, Devon
Half Moon, Cheriton Fitzpaine, Devon
Bottle Inn, Marshwood, Dorset
Chapelhay Tavern, Weymouth, Dorset
Hartcliffe Inn, Hartcliffe, Bristol
Victoria Hotel, Oldfield Park, Bath (currently closed)

Carew Arms, Crowcombe, Somerset
Tuckers Grave, Faulkland, Somerset
Lamb & Fountain, Frome, Somerset
Rose & Crown ('Eli's'), Huish Episcope, Somerset
White Hart, Midsomer Norton, Somerset

Dog & Fox, Bradford-on-Avon, Wiltshire

On an interesting note, the Kings Arms, Stockland (currently closed) has a rare ten-skittle version

Above and below: Chapelhay Tavern, Weymouth (MSS above)

51

Pub listings   **Dorset**

SOMERSET   WILTSHIRE

Shaftesbury

Nether Compton •
• Sherborne

Pamphill

DEVON
Marshwood
Pymore •   • Powerstock   East Morden

Bournemouth
• Bridport

Wareham •

N ↑

Weymouth   Langton Matravers
Worth Matravers •

0   10km

• Easton, Portland

Bournemouth
41 Windham Road, BH1 4RN
01202 551589
Not listed
LPA: Bournemouth

🍺 🍴 (L)

The former private bar

Cricketers ☆

The etching on the windows reveals the layout when this fine pub was rebuilt in Edwardian times. The smoking room, public bar and bottle and jug have since been combined but the private bar at the back remains. The smoking room area, now used for pool, has a decorative door panel, excellent tiling and a striking fireplace. A vestibule with deep-cut 'public bar' panels leads into that former room; notable features include two cast-iron columns with spiral decorations, the old curved bar counter and mirrored bar-backs and benches which came from a local church. The former private bar also has a splendid curved counter and bar-back plus some decorative partitioning. A wide doorway takes you to a baronial-style lounge, originally the billiard room, with an ornamental fireplace and a high mantel shelf. The gents' are well worth a visit for their massive urinals, mosaic tiling and colourful windows.

Bridport

4 South Street, DT6 3NQ
01308 423187
www.thegeorgebridport.co.uk
Grade II listed
LPA: West Dorset
 (L, E)

George Hotel In the centre of town, this 18th-century three-storey former hotel retains a number of Victorian and early 20th-century fittings. The entrance corridor has a colourful tiled floor and a serving hatch (unused) with glazed doors. In the public bar (once two rooms and now extended as well) are an old panelled counter and mostly original bar-back plus an old, tiled, cast-iron fireplace; there is another one in the 'snug', front left.

The public bar – note the 'Jug Dept.' window (MSS)

East Morden

(On B3075), BH20 7DL
01929 459238
www.cockandbottlemorden.co.uk
Grade II listed
LPA: Purbeck
 (L, E)

Cock & Bottle The remarkable little Pat's Happy Chatter's Bar here is the result of a 'theming' exercise carried out in many of their pubs by Hall & Woodhouse brewery in the 1950s and is almost certainly the last remaining example. It has a bare wood floor and, from the refit, a distinctive counter and a large fireplace where brick has been added to an older stone one. There is bench and window seating attached to a panelled dado, a splendid high-backed settle adjacent to the fireplace and a chunky two-seat bench. The bar-back has been altered in more recent years. To the right of the public bar is a small area once part of the former off-sales. Right of the entrance, a separate small lounge has old dado panelling and a small counter front from the 1950s with what is no more than a hatch above (currently filled in by a cabinet). The pub was massively extended to the left around 1990 when a former cellar and garages were replaced by a brick extension to create the new lounge and dining areas.

The Pat's Happy Chatters Bar (Photo courtesy of Cock & Bottle, East Morden)

53

Langton Matravers

27 High Street, BH19 3HA

01929 422979

Grade II listed

LPA: Purbeck

  (L, E)

Kings Arms ☆

The pub rooms here were originally the public bar, rear right, and the smoke room/lounge front left. Around 1960, the present main bar was created in what was the courtyard and a further extension in the 1980s added the small area rear left. The original public bar has an old flagstone floor, dado panelling with wall benches attached and a small counter with old front and modern top. The main bar has changed little in its sixty years – the bar counter and bar-back may be older, having been moved from the public bar. The former smoke room has fitted benches attached to a panelled dado and these and the fireplace could be from the 1950s. The front-right room was the village mortuary until 1943, later becoming the licensee's sitting room until it came into pub use in the mid-1970s.

The main bar little-changed in 60 years

Marshwood

(On B3165), DT6 5QJ

01297 678103

www.bottleinn.co.uk

Grade II Listed

LPA: West Dorset

  (L, E)

The old smoker on the ceiling (MSS)

Bottle Inn An 18th-century thatched and rendered village pub. The main bar has a counter from 1940 and a very old fireplace with Dorset oven – note the rare old smoker in the ceiling, blocked up in 1963. The bar-back dates from that year which is also when the room on the right was converted from private quarters; the fittings are also from this time. The large extension, rear right, followed in the 1980s. The pub hosts the World Nettle Eating Championships in July each year.

The servery with a counter dated 1940 (MSS)

Nether Compton

DT9 4QE
01935 812523
Grade II listed   LPA: West Dorset
🍺

Griffins Head Built 1599 of stone with 19th and 20th-century alterations. On the left, the small lounge bar has a bar counter thought to be from 1947, an old stone inglenook fireplace with a stone seat, a couple of old settles (one imported from a nearby pub) and window seating. Behind the bar is a rare (but unused) Dalex 'signal

lever' handpump (see p.87). The public bar on the right has a flagstone floor and old stone fireplace. Again, the bar counter is likely to be from 1947 but the mosaic mirrored bar-back dates from 1968 as does the creation of the room on the far right and its amalgamation with the public bar.

The left-hand lounge bar
with a counter dated 1947

Pamphill

Vine Hill, BH21 4EE
01202 882259
Not listed
LPA: East Dorset
🍺 🍴 (L)

Vine ★

This delightful little country hostelry became a pub about 1900 when the present landlady's grandfather fitted it out as such. Until the 1950s it sold only beer and cider under a six-day (Mon–Sat) licence. The falling site means it is on two levels. On the lower is the little-altered public bar which, at eight feet square in front of the counter, is one of the country's smallest. Nine steps lead up to the rather larger

tap room, lined with full-height panelling. On the other side of the public bar, a separate entrance leads into the lounge, once the grandfather's sitting room and probably brought into pub use in the 1950s or 1960s. The gents' is outside at the front of the building; the ladies' is also outside but seems to be a relatively late addition. The front garden, overlooked by a prolific vine, is a great place to relax on a warm, sunny day. The pub is owned by the National Trust. Food confined to snacks.

In the tiny public bar

Easton, Portland
133 Reforne, DT5 2AP
01305 820011
Grade II listed
LPA: Weymouth & Portland
🍺 🍴 (L, E; not Mon, Tue)

The King's Shilling Bar with its
partition wall

George Inn ☆

Dated 1765, the George was formerly three houses and later hosted meetings of the Court Leet (a manorial court), becoming a pub around 1840. The original pub, consisting of three small rooms off an L-shaped passageway, is little altered since the 1930s. On the right of the passageway is a small dining room with a 1930s fireplace. The King's Shilling Bar on the left, separated from the passageway by a timber partition with benches attached, has a parquet floor and three fine old tables (one some 8 feet long) but has lost its fireplace. Service was originally via a hatch which was replaced by the present bar counter in the 1970s. At the rear, and slightly opened up from the passageway, is the Reeve Lounge where, hanging on the wall above the fireplace, is the long Portland Reeve Staff which recorded the payment of 'Quit Rent' as a substitute for military service. This small room has a fine 1930s brick fireplace, a parquet floor and dado panelling and is served via a hatch/doorway with a flap across it. In 1995, the Quarr Bar was formed on the left side of the building from a former kitchen and part of the cellar.

Powerstock, DT6 3TF
01308 485328
www.threeshoesdorset.co.uk
Not listed   LPA: West Dorset
🍺

The public bar with its
thatched servery (MSS)

Three Horseshoes ☆

Built in 1906 of brick and stone. The front door leads to a passage with panelled floor and ceiling and a very old double-hinged door to the servery which possibly operated as an off-sales and currently serves customers in the room on the left. This room has old varnished full-height panelling on the walls and also on the ceiling and is now entered through a gap close to the front door – the entrance was further down the passage until recently. A door on the right accesses the public bar where two rooms were combined into one around 1960. It has a plain wood floor, a bar counter that looks earlier in style with thatch above it, floor-to-ceiling panelling around most of the room and a 1960s stone fireplace. The upper bar-back fitting is probably from around 1960; note the small till drawer suspended from the bottom of the main shelf. A further wood-panelled room is entered from the public bar through a short passage opposite the servery; this was being fitted out as a games room at the time of writing (April 2019) and will be accessed by the original (currently shut) front door.

The fully-panelled left-hand room

Pymore
Pymore Road, DT6 5PN
01308 422625
Grade II listed
LPA: West Dorset

 (L)

Pymore Inn ☆

Mid-19th-century stone building converted from a house in around 1950. Originally two rooms with a hall just inside, it became a single lino-floored bar in the 1960s. The canted counter with its beauty-board front is from the original conversion and the bar-back is of glass shelves onto mirrors. Also in the room are brick fireplaces from at latest the 1950s and old dado panelling with some benches attached. A further small room can be found on the left. The pub was due to change hands in mid-2019 with the new owners intending to make improvements – so a check before visiting is advisable.

The 1950s interior (MSS)

Games at the Pub

People go to pubs for pleasure and relaxation so it's not surprising that they have always been venues for playing a multitude of games. Some, like cards, dominoes or that more recent invention, the pub quiz, require no special provision. At the other end of the scale, the likes of long-alley skittles (see feature on p.50) and outdoor bowling demand substantial investment.

The game most associated with pubs is, undoubtedly, darts. Although not as popular as it was 30 or 40 years ago, it's thought to be played regularly by some two million people, with pubs as the prime location for their exertions. A 2006 survey found dartboards in 53% of pubs.

Billiards and snooker have a long association with the pub and many Victorian and Edwardian ones were provided with a purpose-built billiard room.

The baronial-style lounge in the Cricketers, Bournemouth (p.52) was originally such a facility (and there was also one in an upstairs room at the Star, Bath). In the 1930s, bar billiards was introduced into this country and there's a table at the Seymour Arms, Witham Friary, Somerset (p.97). Nowadays, the pool table, which arrived from America in the 1960s, greatly outnumbers its larger billiards cousin in our pubs.

Euchre is a four-player, whist-like card game hugely popular in Devon and Cornwall. Its origins are obscure – some say it came from America with migrant miners, others that it was introduced by French prisoners incarcerated at Dartmoor jail during the Napoleonic wars. One games historian believes it was first played in Alsace and another has found no reference to it being in England before the 1860s. The

The Purbeck Board at the Square & Compass Worth Matravers

rules are too complex to rehearse in any detail here but it's played in competitive pairs with just five cards being dealt to each player, the object being to win at least three of the five tricks. It was the first game in the world to use the joker as a gaming card – it's the highest trump in the Cornish version and known as the 'benny'. In some pubs, euchre can get as noisy as a game of West Indian dominoes and even if you have no clue what's going on, it can make for great entertainment.

Sadly, many outdoor bowling greens have been lost and the only pub featured in this guide that still has one is the Bell on the Common, Broughton Gifford, Wiltshire (p.101). A fair number continue to function in other parts of the country, especially in the North and Midlands.

The card game Euchre being played at the Star, St Just   (Photo by Yanai Sharabi)

Some games are local to the South West or small areas of it – like Purbeck board. This form of shove ha'penny is played on long boards (around 4' 6") and marked not with beds but a target area. The game is played with vintage and now precious wafer-thin coins and, in the 1970s, some fifteen Dorset pubs played the game. Only a handful now do so but the Square & Compass, Worth Matravers, Dorset (p.63), has a board. Thursday nights between October and March used to be when the boards came out – the rest of the time they were stashed away to protect their lovingly-polished surfaces.

The Shoot Room at the Lamb, Devizes (MSS)

The slate shove ha'penny board at the Star, Bath

The more usual version of shove ha'penny can be played on a slate board at the Star, Bath (p.81) where it is always ready for use.

The Devizes area of Wiltshire has a Miniature Rifles League in which local pubs and clubs compete. The Lamb, Devizes (p.102) has a rifle range and shoot room connected with this league. Participants shoot down a specially-made tube which was installed in 1939; it is accessed from a hole in the wall and runs 37 feet down the length of the building.

More details of these and other pub games can be found in a superb book, *Played at the Pub: the Pub Games of Britain* (2009) by Arthur Taylor which is available for just £10 (post free in the UK) from **www.playedinbritain.co.uk**

Shaftesbury

24 Bleke Street, SP7 8JZ
01747 853219
Grade II listed
LPA: North Dorset

Ship ☆

17th-century building, converted to a pub in 1937 when the original Ship Hotel was demolished. In the main bar, the counter has a panelled front and shutters which are believed to work – but nobody dares lower them in case they get stuck! There is a mirrored bar-back and, alongside to the right, another bar-back fitting which may have come from the old Ship – as, almost certainly, did the bell-box on the wall. Opposite the counter is a small area formed by a ceiling-height panelled partition with fixed seating attached. Left of the entrance is the snug with high-backed fitted seating on one side and an old bench on the other. Front left, a latch door leads to the bare-boarded 'Whine Bar', served from a hatch and with dado panelling, some fixed seating and a good carved fireplace. A passage to the right accesses a small bar with a panelled counter and fixed seating. The lower-level area is in an extension into former cottages.

The 1937 bar counter and screen

Sherborne

Cooks Lane, DT9 3NS
01935 813148
www.digbytap.co.uk
Grade II listed
LPA: West Dorset
 (L)

Digby Tap ☆

A 16th/17th-century building, formerly a workhouse, this tucked-away pub has the atmosphere of a genuinely old and little-changed ale house. The front door leads into a part-panelled lobby with a flagstone floor that continues into the passage. At the end of this is a split door that suggests a former off-sales and acts as a serving hatch for the room on the right; the top part of this door is a rare multi-glazed section that can still be closed. As the passage continues to the right, it opens up to a flagstone-floored room with an old stone fireplace but which is likely

Above **The rare intact off-sales**
Right **The front left area** (MSS)

to have come into pub use in later years. Left of the split door is the main bar, which was once two rooms. The front left area has a flagstone floor, old dado panelling with bare benches attached and a stone fireplace. The area in front of the servery was originally accessed from a door near the exterior door. On the counter is a set of 1959 Gaskell & Chambers Dalex handpumps so the counter is at least that old. A doorway at the rear of the main bar leads to another small bar, converted from a cellar in 2014.

Wareham

41 North Street, BH20 4AD
01929 552503
www.kingsarmswareham.co.uk
Grade II listed   LPA: Purbeck
🍺 🍴 (L, E)

Kings Arms 18th-century brick-built thatched pub that retains two of its original three rooms and its passageway layout. Some of the fixtures, like the slatted-wood bar counters, date from changes in the early 1960s. On the left, the characterful public bar has a flagstone floor, inglenook fireplace, an impressive two-sided high back settle and a couple of old benches. On the right-hand side of the passage is the former private bar and a small servery is at the end. The room at the rear right dates from the 1990s.

The main bar

Weymouth
High West Street, DT4 8JH
07809 440772
Grade II listed
LPA: Weymouth & Portland

Boot Inn ☆

Although the building itself dates to the early-17th century, the room layout and many of the fittings are from a 1930s refit. The small bare-boarded corner 'Saloon Bar' has a counter that pre-dates the refit (note the now-defunct Victorian water tap), dado panelling with benches and a period fireplace. Up two steps at the back is a tiny

snug with one panelled wall and service from a hatch/doorway. On the left, the bare-boarded public bar was once two rooms and has an inter-war counter and dado panelling but a more recent bar-back. This room has been extended into former living quarters fairly recently.

The saloon bar with the snug on the right and public bar ahead

Weymouth
34 Franchise Street, DT4 8JU
01305 786811
Not listed
LPA: Weymouth & Portland

Chapelhay Tavern A 19th-century building that was originally two cottages then a pub with four small rooms. The front bar has a canted inter-war bar counter, some old bar-back shelving and some possibly pre-war dado panelling. Off to the left, the small area was once a separate room and the folding wooden screen may have replaced a wall. A pool table and then skittle alley lie beyond. The rear bar, with full-height ply panelling, was enlarged in 1973 and the bar fittings are quite recent.

The front bar (MSS)

Worth Matravers, BH19 3LF
01929 439229
www.squareandcompasspub.co.uk
Grade II listed   LPA : Purbeck
🍺 🍎 🍴 (L, E)

Square & Compass ★

This renowned pub, established in the late-18th century, has been run by the Newman family since 1907. Picturesquely situated on the world-famous Jurassic Coast, it has stunning views out to sea and is also one of only five pubs to have appeared in every edition of the *Good Beer Guide* since it was first published in 1974. A flagstone passage leads to a servery/cellar at the back where service is via a hatch/doorway (this is a rare example of a no-counter pub.) To the left is a further hatch then wooden partition walls mark out the venerable tap room, entered by a (once) sliding door. This too has a flagstone floor plus solid benches and a large fireplace (opened up in 1990 and a wood-burning stove installed). To the right is the 'Big Room' which was a small parlour before 1935 when it was extended into the stable block, hence the different ceiling heights. It is fitted with a continuous wood-block floor, fielded panelling and, on the left, a hatch for service (the big opening behind the curtains is from 1978). The pub still has outside toilets and sells as much real cider as beer. A museum of local fossils is housed in a room to the left. Food confined to pies and pasties.

The venerable tap room

Cider and Perry

"Everybody thinks I drink beer but I actually like cider!"

PRINCE WILLIAM

The South West is well known for cider production and there is evidence of cider being produced from the fermented juice of crab apples as far back as Roman times. The common varieties used in the area today are bitter sweets and bitter sharps such as Kingston Black, Collogett Pippin, Dabinett and Somerset Redstreak.

Until the middle of the last century, cider represented more than mere refreshment in the region. It was a vital part of the rural economy and it was accepted that casual farm labourers would be partly paid in drink. It was used as local barter, with almost every farm operating a press and farmers would place flagons at either end of the field during harvest, in the hope that it would spur work with labourers rationed up to eight pints per day during harvest time. Imagine consuming a gallon of cider and trying to do a desk job!

Ye Olde Cider Bar, Newton Abbot, one of the last remaining cider pubs in the country

Truly a testament to the sobering nature of hard manual labour and sweat.

Nowadays, the majority of the cider available in pubs is artificially carbonated and comes from larger producers. The good news is that there are increasing numbers of smaller producers around the country, including many in the South West. Their production methods are less industrial and many use local produce, resulting in a still product where the taste of the apples used comes bursting through.

This guide includes one of the few cider houses left in the country, Ye Olde Cider Bar in Newton Abbot (p.44), which was CAMRA's National Cider Pub of the Year in 2011. Cider houses were in essence pubs that only sold cider (no beer) and, until recent times, were common in English counties in the West and South West, but now only a handful are left in the whole country.

Other pubs in this guide renowned for their dedication to a range of real ciders and perries are another winner of the National Cider Pub of the Year title, The Square & Compass in Worth Matravers, Dorset (p.63), which won this accolade in 2008, Tucker's Grave in Faulkland, (p.88), and the Seymour Arms, Witham Friary (p.97), both Somerset.

It's great to see the increasing number of cider producers and more real cider and perry being available in our pubs but they need our support, so if you see a 'cider for sale' sign pointing down an old farm track, turn off. If you see real cider available in a pub, give it a try.

Tucker's Grave, Faulkland sells as much cider as beer

More information on Real Cider and Perry is available on CAMRA's website (**www.camra.org.uk/cider**).

'Real cider' is a term used to describe traditional cider made from freshly pressed apples. Served still rather than force carbonated, real cider is unpasteurised during production and not micro-filtered to produce a truly natural and delicious alcoholic drink. Perry is produced in the same way but is made from pears.

The Seymour Arms, Witham Friary

Gloucestershire and Bristol

Ampney St Peter, GL7 5SL
Grade II listed   LPA : Cotswold

Red Lion ★

Closed at the time of writing – *see* Closed Pubs (p.110)

Bristol: City Centre
60 Victoria Street, BS1 6DE
0117 929 2338
Grade II listed
LPA: Bristol

Kings Head ★

The long, narrow building plot no doubt echoes a medieval site but the present building dates back to the mid-17th-century. Inside, the bar stretches right back to a rear entrance facing the bombed-out late-medieval Temple Church which has been nick-named 'the Leaning Tower of Bristol' as it leans one degree more than the one in Pisa. Along the right-hand wall is a magnificent marble-shelved mid-Victorian bar-back with a series of arches and high-level lettering advertising various drinks. Dated 1865, it is the second oldest bar-back we know about (that at the Victoria, Bayswater W2 pre-dates it by a year). The panelled counter is no doubt part of the same scheme but has a recent top. Most of the back part of the pub comprises the delightful 'Tramcar Bar' – a snug supposedly shaped like an old tramcar.

The Tramcar Bar, so named due to its shape

Its insertion, presumably around the turn of the 20th century, led to the counter being cut back, hence the 'stranded' bar-back in this area. Until then, other than the small seated area at the front, this was presumably a largely stand-up drinking establishment. Not to be missed are the glazed panel advertising 'Burton Ales and Dublin Stout' and the old pressure gauge from gas lighting days. Two gas fittings survive in the Tramcar Bar as do four converted to electricity in the servery. The two tiny WCs adjacent to the rear wall are formed by part-glazed partitions – note the 'Ladies Only' on the glass door panel.

The interior showing the bar fittings that date back to 1865

Bristol: Hartcliffe

Brooks Road, BS13 0HQ

0117 941 0251

Not listed

LPA: Bristol

Hartcliffe Inn ☆

A mostly untampered-with 1958 estate pub; although the utilitarian design won't be to everyone's taste, few interiors of this vintage have escaped later 'improvement'. The long, narrow public bar has lost a partition half way down so opens directly on to the remarkable in-pub skittle alley. The counters and bar-backs are original – the second one was initially used for food service. The fireplace is a recent insertion. The smaller lounge is completely intact with padded panelled counter, classic period bar-back, bench seating on two sides, plywood dado, coloured stone fireplace and even the original carpet! Upstairs is the assembly room, not presently in use.

The unaltered 1958 lounge (MSS)

Bristol: Hotwells

Nova Scotia Place, BS1 6XJ

0117 929 7994

Grade II listed

LPA: Bristol

(L, E)

Nova Scotia ☆

A late-19th-century pub converted from a row of three terraced houses. It retains its mahogany bar-back fitting with a door to an office in the middle – imaginative legend says it was made for a ship but didn't fit so was installed here instead. However, the remarkable survivor here is the Victorian low screen, attached to the ceiling with an iron stay, situated to the right of the public bar. This creates the small snug known as the Captain's Cabin with etched glass stating that in previous times it was a 'Private Bar'. Old bench seating is attached to panelled walls throughout the pub. The area on the left was once a separate room.

The interior showing the rare Victorian low screen (on the right)

Bristol: Kingsdown

164 St. Michael's Hill, BS2 8DE
0117 973 3203
www.highburyvaults.co.uk
Not listed
LPA: Bristol

🍺 🍴 (L, E)

Highbury Vaults ☆

A mid-19th-century pub with a narrow frontage. At the front is a lovely, tiny snug with a Victorian counter and mirrored bar-back plus dado panelling, bench seating painted dark green and a fine set of 1936 handpumps. Inner doors lead into a passage with a split door (which perhaps served as an off-sales), panelled dado and wall benches. The rear bar has an inter-war counter, old bar-back fitting and panelled dado. In the early 1980s, a sympathetic extension added another two rooms. Rumour has it that prisoners would have their last meal here before meeting their maker on the gallows at the top of St Michael's Hill.

The tiny snug at the front

The rear bar

Bristol: St George
Blackworth Road, BS5 8AS

Bristol: St Philip's
1–2 West Street, BS2 0DF

Bristol: Southville
185–7 Coronation Road, BS3 1RF
0117 9872431
Not listed
LPA: Bristol

Three Crowns ☆
Closed at the time of writing – *see* Closed Pubs (p.110)

Palace Hotel ☆
Closed at the time of writing – *see* Closed Pubs (p.111)

Avon Packet ☆

Built in 1843, with a tiled frontage added around 1900, this delightfully eccentric pub retains three of its original five rooms and many old fittings. From the entrance, you are standing in a passage which led to the back of the pub with the bar area on your left and the former parlour on the right, both with fixed seating – the separating walls were removed in the 1970s. The panelled bar counter, with consoles along the front, seems to have been shortened and possibly moved as well. Behind the servery, the barman's exit also acts as a serving hatch. The former parlour has a decorated cast-iron fireplace with tiles in front. This side of the public bar once housed a bottle and jug. Before you reach the rooms at the back, passageways go both left and right – the former, called 'Bull Shit Corner' has a portable seat facing the serving hatch. Continuing to the rear, you come to what were the smoke room (left) and tap room (right) – again the separating walls have gone. The latter has fixed seating round the walls and a grand cast-iron fireplace. A pit in the garden is said to have been used for bear-baiting – somewhat unlikely given that bear-baiting was prohibited in 1835.

The servery (MSS)

Cranham, GL4 8HP
01452 812217
Not listed
LPA: Stroud
 (E)

Black Horse ☆

17th-century pub almost hidden up a side road with two small rooms that have not changed in over fifty years. The public bar on the left has a red quarry tiled floor and old dado panelling all round the walls with bare benches attached. The style of the Formica-topped counter suggests it was installed in the 1950s/early 1960s – the bar-back

shelves could be of similar age. The lounge on the right, through a narrow door and down two steps, has a bar-back with an illuminated panel at the top and glass shelves of a style seen with refits circa 1960, which is probably also the date of the counter. Two small rooms upstairs have been brought into use as dining rooms – the first has 'beauty board' dado panelling. The car park is situated further up the hill, past the pub.

The public bar with a 1950s counter

Ford, GL54 5RU
01386 594215
www.theploughinnford.co.uk
Grade II listed
LPA: Cotswold
 (L, E)

Plough ☆

Stone-built Cotswold inn constructed in the late 17th or early 18th century with an extension dated 1905 on the front gable. The front door leads into a small stone-flagged corridor; behind the door is an old 'bars up', a piece of wood which pulls from the wall to secure the door. Straight ahead is the main bar with a small drinking area in front; the

counter and tiling are post-war but the bar-back shelving is older. To the right, a superb stone-walled, flagstoned room has a beamed ceiling and an old fireplace with modern log burner. The bar counter is a later insertion but doesn't intrude too badly. Old window bench seating is painted cream and the windows have old wooden shutters. The areas to the left of the entrance corridor have suffered much opening out and there are extensions into rooms not formerly in pub use.

The flagstoned right-hand room

Lawrence Weston
Barrowmead Drive, BS11 0JT
07548 257863
Not listed   LPA: Bristol

Giant Goram   Built in 1959 for Simonds Brewery and retaining two of the original three rooms plus skittle alley, making it a rare post-war survival. As with the Hartcliffe, Bristol (p. 67), the plain fittings may seem austere and even uninviting to modern eyes but interiors like this remind us 'how we were' and do possess a simple dignity. The public bar once had moveable screens to partition it off from the Skittles Bar at the back and the alley itself. There are unfussy panelled counters and original bar-backs both here and in the simply-appointed lounge. The skittle alley is presently being used for a kids' bike project but is intact. The off-licence was long ago converted to a kitchen area.

The lounge (MSS)

May Hill, GL17 0NN
01422 830529
www.glasshouselodges.co.uk
Not listed
LPA: Forest of Dean

Glasshouse Inn ☆

Originally, the pub consisted of the two front rooms with a passageway running down the middle with wooden partition walls. The front left 'Smoke Room' with a red quarry-tiled floor has lost its partition wall but an antique settle and some timbers now make it look like a separate room. The 'Public Bar', front right, retains most of its partition wall though markings on the quarry-tiled floor show it to be some two feet shorter. This small room has a tongue-and-groove ceiling, old dado panelling, an old settle and a basic bench. The next room, on the right

The front-right public bar

71

of the original passage, was the living room and has lost its partition wall as indicated by the markings in the quarry-tiled floor. This room was possibly brought into use in the 1950s when the cellar on the left was converted into a servery (there had previously been no counters). On the right is a range fireplace and a tongue-and-groove dado with wall benches plus scrubbed tables and low basic benches. Beyond the servery, an extension was added in 1988 but looks much older.

Newland, GL16 8NP
01594 833260
www.theostrichinn.com
Grade II listed
LPA: Forest of Dean
 (L, E)

Ostrich ☆

A late 17th-century inn last refitted in the 1950s and little changed since. A flagstone passageway runs from the front door to the rear. To the left, the main bar, which would have been two small rooms in the distant past, has a very large old stone fireplace with huge lintel. The bar counter was installed in the 1950s (the bar-back shelves look more recent) and other features include the dado panelling with bench seating attached, two curved high-backed settles, shutters on the windows and a characterfully 'lumpy' ceiling (can you spot the sheep?). On the right of the passage is a small dining room which would also once have been two very small rooms. Outside gents' and ladies' at the rear.

The main bar with a 1950s bar counter

Prestbury
Mill Street, GL52 3BG
01242 361506
www.theploughprestbury.co.uk
Grade II listed
LPA: Cheltenham
  (L, E)

Plough Inn ☆

This 17th/early-18th-century thatched pub comprises two little changed rooms and an L-shaped passage. To the left is a splendid room with uneven pale-coloured flagstone floor, large stone fireplace with log fire, and tongue and groove panelling around the walls – full-height on the rear and half-height on the front – with fixed seating attached to it. A full-height partition with a door in the middle formerly divided the room but only the left-hand part remains. The quoits and an old scorer on the wall, two scrubbed tables and a grandfather clock add to the atmosphere. Service comes from the hatch at the end of the rear right-hand passage. The lounge to the right of the entrance door was last altered around 1960 when the small hatch/counter was added

The left-hand room

by creating a hole in the wall. The bar-back cabinetwork in three sections also dates from this time but the brick fireplace is a little earlier and the fixed seating is from 2003.

Purton
Over the canal bridge, GL13 9HU
Not listed
LPA: Stroud

Berkeley Arms ('Ted Lord's') ★

About 200 yards from the lift bridge over the Gloucester & Sharpness Canal and with great views out to the River Severn, here we have a no frills, unspoilt rural pub still with a smallholding. Historically, pubs were often combined with other businesses but nowadays this is a

The barely-altered main room

real rarity. The central section was extended in the mid-19th century. You enter to a tiny drinking area with a quarry-tiled floor and a bench beneath the window. The servery has an old counter and shelves. Beyond on the left, a separate room has a flagstone floor, large curved high-backed settle, large stone fireplace and a hatch to the side of the servery. The only recent change was the building of indoor toilets in the 1960s. Closed October to Easter. Opens 7pm, also noon to 2pm, Sat. & Sun.

Shortwood
Main Road, BS16 9NG
Not listed
LPA: South Gloucestershire
🍺 🍴 (L, E)

Bridge Stone-built 1880s drinkers' pub. On the left, the U-shaped bar was two rooms separated by a partition wall removed around 1980 – there is also an extension into a previously non-public area. The fine old, probably Victorian, counter survives but the bar-back fitting is reputed to have come from the nearby closed station. Until recently, behind the part-glazed screen near the entrance was a superb 'Outdoor Dept' that also acted as a snug where some customers drank but it is now a store cupboard. The lounge has been modernised in the last few years. Food confined to pies, pasties and rolls.

The interior showing the rare partitioned 'Outdoor Dept.'

Tewkesbury
8 Church Street, GL20 5PA
01684 293034
www.berkeleyarms.pub
Grade II* listed
LPA: Tewkesbury
🍺 🍴 (L, E)

Berkeley Arms An early 16th-century timber-framed three-storey twin-gabled building. Both front and rear bars contain several 1930s features – panelled counters, bar-backs with mirrors and ribbed glass and brick fireplaces. A blue-brick passage runs down the right-hand side with entrances off it to the rear bar and outside gents'. Behind is a former warehouse (c.1600) which has been converted into a dining/ meeting room with open rafters.

The servery in the front bar

Winterbourne, Watley's End
North Road, BS36 1PT
01454 850378
www.themasonspub.co.uk
Not Listed
LPA: South Gloucestershire
🍺 🍴 (L, E)

Masons Arms ☆

A two-storey 1880s-built community pub with single-storey extensions to left and right. Originally there was just one bar in the middle but, in the late 1950s, George's Bristol Brewery carried out a refurbishment – little has changed since. The lounge on the left is the original pub room extended to the left by incorporating a store room. It has a counter with a classic 1950s front, mirrored bar-back and dado panelling on the walls painted bright red. The only changes are the blocking-up of a fireplace left of the counter and the metal pot-shelf. Note the original front door in the bay. The public bar on the right was a private living room until the revamp and has a plainer counter front, period bar-back fitting, more bright red dado panelling and a tiled and minimal wood surround fireplace – even the original display case remains.

The public bar on the right (MSS)

Why no mention of...?

Readers of this book familiar with the South West might know of genuinely old pubs which aren't covered in our listings and be asking 'why not?'. As a rule, the reason is that our concern is with **interiors** and many old pubs have been much altered inside – which isn't to say that they aren't still precious.

A classic example is the George, Norton St Philip, Somerset – externally, arguably the country's best preserved coaching inn. This Grade I listed building was begun in the 14th century (and extended over the next couple of centuries) by the Carthusian monks at nearby Hinton Charterhouse. It provided accommodation for travellers attending their annual wool fair and doubled as a wool store. Four rooms – two used as a bar and lounge and two for dining – have been in continuous inn use for centuries. The building is structurally intact with its thick stone walls, corridors, massive beams and enormous fireplaces. In the centre, a delightful cobbled courtyard is overlooked by a gallery leading to hotel bedrooms. However, there is no getting away from the fact that many, if not most, of the internal fittings are either recent or recently imported – bar counters, bar-backs, doors, panelling and so on.

The New Inn, Gloucester, also listed Grade I, is our finest example of a medieval galleried inn and, standing in the central courtyard, you get a true sense of the place's long history. Sadly, all the bars and other internal spaces have been substantially refitted with nothing of note later than the 1970s. There are, of course, lots of timber-framed walls, posts and beams but little 'pubby' that is of any age, which is what matters for this book.

Glastonbury in Somerset has an ancient pilgrims' inn, the George & Pilgrims, built between 1455 and 1475 by Abbot Selwood to accommodate visitors to the abbey. It claims to be the oldest purpose-built pub in the region. The three-storey building has a highly decorative facade resembling a small castle with its battlements, mullioned windows and stone-carved shields.

The George, Norton St Philip is a Grade I-listed building dating back to the 14th century

The interior of the George & Pilgrims, Glastonbury

The present bar occupies what were two rooms, the dividing wall being removed probably in the 1950s. It has wonderful oak walls on the passage side but there is also much modern woodwork. Opening up between this room and the corridor and between the corridor and the room on the right (also two joined together) means the whole layout is significantly changed. The bar counter and some of the bar-back looks to be from the late 1950s.

Another fine courtyard inn is the Red Lion, Milford Street, Salisbury. The courtyard itself is cobbled and is home to what is believed to be Europe's oldest hanging creeper. Once inside you soon come across several world-famous clocks including a skeleton/organ clock whose case was carved by prisoners of war captured after the defeat of the Spanish Armada. The residents' lounge has an impressive carved wood-surround fireplace and an attractive corner settle – but most 'pub' fittings here and in the bar are of no age or distinction.

Should you come across a South West pub and find yourself baffled as to why we haven't included it in this book, then do please get in touch (**info@ pubheritage.camra.org.uk**). If we've checked it out and decided it doesn't meet our criteria, then we can tell you why. If it's one we simply haven't investigated, then we'll be very grateful for the lead.

The skeleton clock at the Red Lion, Salisbury

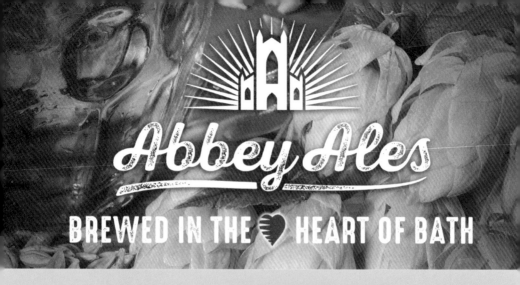

BREWED IN THE ❤ HEART OF BATH

With a Choice of Great Pubs in Bath city centre

Star INN

23 Vineyards, Bath BA1 5NA
Tel 01225 425072

THE ASSEMBLY INN

16 Alfred Street, Bath BA1 2QU
Tel 01225 333639

COEUR DE LION

17 Northumberland Place, Bath
BA1 5AR Tel 01225 463568

www.abbeyales.co.uk

The Abbey Brewery
Camden Row, Bath BA1 5LB
Tel 01225 444437

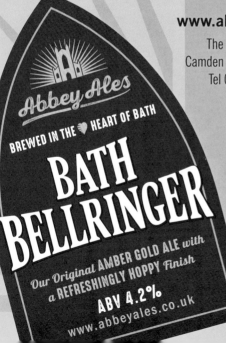

BREWED IN THE ❤ HEART OF BATH

BATH BELLRINGER

Our Original AMBER GOLD ALE with a REFRESHINGLY HOPPY Finish

ABV 4.2%

www.abbeyales.co.uk

BREWED IN THE HEART

BATH BEST *Bitter*

www.abbeyales.co.uk

ABV 4.0%

The Abbey Brewery Somerset

Somerset

GLOUCESTERSHIRE
& BRISTOL

- Clapton-in-Gordano
- Nailsea
- Keynsham
- Kelston
- Bath
- Weston-super-Mare
- Faulkland
- Emborough
- Midsomer Norton
- Priddy
- Frome
- Porlock
- Dunster
- Witham Friary
- Crowcombe
- Huish Episcopi
- Appley

DEVON

N

DORSET

0   10km

Appley, TA21 0HJ
01823 673147
www.theappleyglobe.co.uk
Grade II listed
LPA: Taunton Deane
🍺 🍴 (L, E)

Globe 17th-century pub, formerly cottages, that has retained its three-room plan and some of its 19th-century fittings. From the front porch, which has fixed bench seating, a long, narrow, brick-floored corridor runs through the pub. The original public room is the brick-floored 'Men's Kitchen' (cf Rose & Crown, Huish Episcopi) on the left with matchboard dado panelling, fixed bench seating and a 1930s brick fireplace; the settle is a modern replacement for a much older one. An opening has been cut through to another old room to the rear, again with matchboard dado panelling though this has recently been reduced in height. The right-hand room has largely modern fittings. Across the corridor is a small Victorian bar counter with glazed top section but this is no longer in use.

The front left-hand 'Men's Kitchen' room (MSS)

Bath: centre

1 York Street, BA1 1NG
01225 571070
Grade II listed
LPA: Bath & North East Somerset
🍺 🍴 (L)

Alehouse ☆

Built around 1816, the pub once consisted of the small public bar, an off-sales in the passage behind and a lounge at the rear which is now the beer cellar. The public bar retains its splendid decoratively carved and mirrored bar-back with a small return in the corner; it has been painted mauve. The upper shelves are held up by slender columns with decorative capitals, below which about two-thirds of the old bar shelves survive (the remainder removed for a fridge). The bar counter (painted bright purple) is from late Victorian times and has decorative brackets. All round the walls is old dado panelling with benches round the windows. In the passage behind the servery you can still see the former off-sales hatch with two small leaded windows. There is also a cellar bar with several vaulted rooms, but no old fittings. Upstairs, a small pool room has been brought into use and another room converted into a kitchen.

The public bar with its
Victorian bar fittings (MSS)

Bath: centre

12 Green Street, BA1 2JZ
01225 448259
Grade II listed
LPA: Bath & North East Somerset
🍺 🍴 (L)

Old Green Tree ★

The building here is 18th-century but was extended backwards in 1926 and refurbished in a pleasingly restrained fashion by local architect, W. A. Williams, who also designed the shop-like frontage. The plan is one regularly found in the north of the country but rare in the south. Rooms are each side of the servery which has, in front of it, a drinking lobby acting as the public bar. All these spaces are panelled and have herringbone wood-block floors (carpeted at the front). The small lounge left of the entrance has service via a doorway to the servery – there is a similar arrangement in the smoke room at the back. All doors still bear the numbers used to identify the rooms for licensing purposes ('1' on the lounge door, '2' on the front bar, '3' on the smoke room and '4' on the cellar door). The gents', down eleven steps, retains its 1926 urinals.

The small, panelled rear smoke room

Bath: centre

23 The Vineyards, Paragon,
BA1 5NA   01225 425072

www.abbeyinnsbath.co.uk/
#the-star-inn-bath

Grade II listed

LPA: Bath & North East Somerset

Star ★

The Star occupies a Georgian terrace and was first licensed in the 1760s. What we see today is a wonderful survival from a refitting in 1928, when the pub was extended into half of no.22 next door by architect W. A.Williams (cf the Old Green Tree). It has scarcely altered since and consists of four rooms and an entrance lobby. On the left is an attractive panelled lounge, still with bell-pushes. To the right is a small snug with a long bench whose popularity with elderly customers has earned it the soubriquet 'Death Row'. Note the vintage telephone positioned so that it could be used by both customers and staff.

The servery with casks on stillage

The 'Glass Room', a name only seen in Bath

A timber screen separates the snug from the 'Glass Room', which has a fold-up slate shove ha'penny board. Finally comes the screened-off public bar in front of the servery where two casks of Bellringer are stillaged. This is the only pub in the South West using a very traditional way to serve beer – from the cask into a jug and then from the jug to your glass. Note the annunciator box at the back of the servery. The Star serves as the brewery tap for Abbey Ales of Bath.

Bath: Larkhall
St Saviour's Road, BA1 6SD
01225 425710   Grade II listed
LPA: Bath & North East Somerset

Larkhall Inn ☆

The Larkhall Inn occupies a handsome mid-18th-century building and contains several late-Victorian features. You enter by a small intact vestibule into the public bar which, though large, always seems to have been one space. Sitting on the Victorian bar counter are three

The public bar with its Victorian bar counter

non-operational handpumps dated 1887. The bar-back fittings are later but still mostly of some age. Elsewhere in this room are a parquet floor, old dado panelling, fine lengths of bench seating and an impressive stone fireplace. To the left of the entrance, opening out into a lower level has taken place, with more tampering further back to create an open staircase. Note the old partition/draught screen by the door to the private quarters. A small pool room at the front has a parquet floor and hatch for service.

Bath: Oldfield Park
Millmead Road, BA2 3JW

Victoria Hotel
Closed at the time of writing – *see* Closed Pubs (p.111)

Bath: Twerton
Poolemead Road, BA2 1QR
01225 332160
Grade II listed
LPA: Bath & North East Somerset

Centurion Inn ☆
Built in 1965 and remarkably little-altered since, the striking design of this pub owes much to its hillside position. The exposed site is also the reason why an unusual system of pressurisation, linked to the central heating and ventilation system, was installed – note the distinctive doors. From the car park, you enter a lobby with a terrazzo floor and a store room on the right. The skittle alley was converted from a garage, store and part of the cellar in the late 1970s/early

The 1965 lounge bar

1980s. A terrazzo staircase leads to the entrance hall with numerous doors, including those to the main bars. The lounge is on the left and has a balustraded higher level for darts. The original counter is in a distinct period style with a Formica front and top and the mirrored bar-back is also intact. Up a step is the former Buttery area, once separated with a partition, and with a suspended ceiling of hollow steel laths. Again, the counter is original, part panelled and part Formica-fronted plus a black Formica top. Down the left hand side is a mirrored display case – this was originally a food-serving area and has lost its counter. The walls are lined with timber panelling and the large windows give great views over Bath. The same applies in the public bar on the right. This also has a raised, balustraded darts area and similar counters and bar-backs. A door leads to a paved patio which wraps round the building. Note the Roman figurines inside and out and the fragment of mosaic displayed in the entrance hall.

Clapton-in-Gordano
Clevedon Lane, BS20 7RH
01275 842105
www.blackhorseclapton.co.uk
Grade II listed
LPA: North Somerset
 (L)

Black Horse ☆

The main bar here was originally subdivided – markings on the red tiled floor indicate the loss of partition walls in the mid-1980s which previously formed a tiny snug in front of the large stone fireplace and also a separate darts area. Down the side of the bar is a separate narrow room with a lino-tiled floor which at one time was the village lock-up – note the iron bars in the rear window. This has a small counter which sometime in the past 30 years replaced an earlier simple affair, as the old photo on the wall shows. The dado panelling on the walls is old and there are some carved wooden settles (and a collection of china pots hanging from the ceiling). A room across the corridor was brought into use in recent times.

The left-hand room, once the village lock-up

Crowcombe, TA4 4AD
01984 618631
www.thecarewarms.co.uk
Grade II listed
LPA: West Somerset
 (L, E)

Carew Arms ☆

Mid-18th-century inn which was enlarged in the early and mid-19th-century. The uneven flagstoned entrance passage has, on one side, a door with a shelf which may have been associated with an off-sales. Front left is the unchanged public bar with old flagstone floor, some tongue-and-groove panelling, a high-backed settle, a long basic bench down one side and two scrubbed tables. The huge stone fireplace was revealed in 1999 when a small one in front was removed. Beyond a wooden partition is the servery with basic, simple shelving and a hatch which was enlarged in 1999. Across the passage, a small room converted from private accommodation is now in occasional use as an overflow dining room. The lounge at the rear has a small post-war counter and in 1999 was doubled in size. The former skittle alley was converted into a dining room with a new bar counter and bar-back fitting added. A new alley has been created from former stables.

The unchanged public bar

Dunster
36 High Street, TA24 6SG
01634 821555
www.luttrellarms.co.uk
Grade II* listed
LPA: West Somerset

  (L, E)

The main bar at the rear

Luttrell Arms Hotel ☆

An imposing late medieval building. From the hotel entrance, a very old partition wall is on the left, behind which is the lounge with a 17th-century plaster ceiling. The small public bar appears to have fittings from the 1950s – bar counter, bar-back and settle seating down the left hand side. The main bar, at the back, has heavy oak ceiling beams, a big old stone fireplace and a small high-backed settle. The counter, with fielded-panelling, may date from 1929 but the copper top is later; the bar-back is mostly modern. A couple of other rooms have come into pub use only recently.

Dispensing Differently

In most pubs, the journey of your pint of real ale from cellar to glass is straightforward. You go to the bar counter and place your order then a handpump is pulled to fill your glass. The South West, though, is rich in pubs where things are done a bit differently.

For a start, here we find one third of the nation's pubs which have never had a bar counter. In times gone by, this was the arrangement in all alehouses, reflecting the domestic origins of our pubs. Counters only began to arrive in the early 19th century, bringing an element of professionalism to the sales process. Our two survivors are the Rose & Crown, Huish Episcopi (p.91) and Tucker's Grave Inn, Faulkland (p.88), both in Somerset. Both are great pubs in their own right but the experience of buying a drink without anything passing over a counter or hatch is not to be missed. Until it closed a few years ago, the single-roomed Red Lion, Ampney St Peter, Gloucestershire (p.110) was another 'no counter' pub; there is a fair chance it may reopen

The cellar area where you are served at the 'no-bar' Rose & Crown ('Eli's'), Huish Episcope

Beer is drawn from the cask at the Square & Compass, Worth Matravers and served through a couple of hatches

and even if this is in expanded form, the original room is likely to be preserved given that the building is statutorily listed.

Other pubs have service methods not greatly different. At the Square & Compass, Worth Matravers, Dorset (p.63), and Drewe Arms, Drewsteignton, Devon (p.37), beer is stored in the cellar, served straight from the cask and passed to the customer through a hatch. Although the Bridge, Topsham, Devon (p.48), has a counter, they prefer to fetch beer from the cellar and place it on a tray or ledge for service (fetching from the cellar also happens at the Royal Inn, Horsebridge, Devon (p.40). The Rugglestone Inn, Widecombe-in-the-Moor, Devon (p.49), had no bar until 1993 and still sells beer from the cask.

Indeed, dispensing ale straight from the cask is a happily common sight in the region. The New Inn, Tynwardreath, Cornwall (p.31), has

sold Draught Bass in this way for donkey's years while the same beer is served from a rare 1970s electric pump dispenser at the Avon Packet, Bristol (p.69). At least seventeen other pubs in this guide continue to use the gravity method of dispense – a row of casks stillaged behind the bar is always a welcome sight and, fortunately, today's in-cask coolers largely guarantee a quality pint.

A very old, but now rare, way to serve real ale is to draw a quantity into a big jug then pour from that into your glass – the Star, Bath (p.81) serves an Abbey beer in this manner.

At the Star, Bath they still serve Abbey Bellringer in the very traditional way – from the cask to a jug and from the jug to your gl

Rare 'signal lever' handpumps at the Rose & Crown ('Eli's'), Huish Episcope

The handpumps are unusually situated on the bar back at the Haunch of Venison, Salisbury which also has a rare set of spirit cocks

Handpumps are the customary dispense method nowadays but not all are of the standard Angram variety. Only three examples are known of 'signal lever' pumps and two are in the South West. The Rose & Crown, Huish Episcopi (p.91), still uses theirs but the one at the

Equally rare 'cash register' handpumps in use at the Old Crown, Kelston

Griffin's Head, Nether Compton, Dorset (p.55), is out of commission. Cash register handpumps are also a rarity and, until recently, only one set was known to be in use – at the Old Crown, Kelston, Somerset (p.92). There are now two other examples – a set brought back into use at the Prince of Wales, Holcombe Rogus, Devon, (not in this guide) and in a Kent micropub.

Pumps invariably live on the counter but at the Haunch of Venison, Salisbury, Wiltshire (p.107), they are attached to the bar-back (the pub also has a rare set of gravity-fed spirit cocks – there are only four examples in the country). The oldest pumps we've found are at the Larkhall Inn, Bath (p.82), dated 1887, though they aren't in use. Also worthy of note is the fine pewter base on which sit the set of handpulls at the Ship, Porlock, Somerset (p.95)

The oldest handpumps in the South West are these disused ones at Larkhall Inn, Larkhall, Bath

The handpumps at the Ship, Porlock are situated on a rare pewter base

Emborough

(On B3139), BA3 4SA
01761 232398
www.theolddowninn.co.uk
Not listed
LPA: Mendip

The small rear bar

Old Down Inn ☆

The star attraction at this large roadside hotel is the delightful small bar at the back. It appears to have been fitted out between the wars and has a small servery with an L-shaped counter and ornamented copper top. The walls are lined with imitation wood panelling (a common embellishment in inter-war pubs giving an antique effect at low cost). Note the sliding hatch to the cross-wise corridor. The numerous other public rooms are all either very plain or modernised. The main bar, rear left, has casks stillaged at the back of the servery.

Faulkland

Wells Road, (A366), BA3 5XF
01373 834230
www.tuckersgraveinn.co.uk
Grade II listed
LPA: Mendip

Tucker's Grave Inn ★

This remarkable three-roomed pub lies on the main road a mile east of Faulkland village. It occupies part of an 18th-century cottage which has housed a pub for over 200 years. The strange name comes from Edwin Tucker, who killed himself in 1747 and was buried nearby (suicides were commonly buried in unconsecrated ground, often

The tap room

No bar counter!

near a crossroads). There is no bar here, the casks of beer and cider being stacked in the bay window of the public bar. To the right is the splendidly unspoilt tap room: the Georgian-style lettering on the door has a claim to be the earliest pub lettering in the country. A third room, far left, formerly a living room, was brought into use in 1985. At the end of the passage, a door leads to the outside toilets at the rear right of the building. A skittle alley is in a separate stone building at the back. A function room is being added on the site (as at May 2019).

Frome

24 Keyford, BA11 1JW
01373 453527
Grade II listed
LPA: Mendip

Crown Inn ☆

Late-17th-century building housing a classic small town pub with two little rooms either side of a central servery and an off-licence between them. The latter still sees some use (mostly to sell cigarette papers!) and has a Victorian counter front and full-height panelling. The smoke room on the right combined two even smaller rooms in the 1990s but old dado panelling with benches and an Art Deco fireplace survive from the former snug. The left-hand public bar fittings look to date mostly from the 1950s/60s – lino-tiled floor, ribbed hardboard counter with Formica top and a bar-back with Formica shelves.

Crown Inn: the left-hand public bar

Frome

57 Castle Street, BA11 3BW
01373 463414
Grade II listed
LPA: Mendip

The very small public bar (MSS)

Lamb & Fountain ('Mothers') ☆

Late-17th or early-18th-century pub, retaining three small rooms. From the front door a passage runs to the rear and halfway down on the left is the off-sales hatch with a sliding glazed window with display case above. The door at the front left leads to a very small public bar with a Victorian counter with a later Formica top; the bar-back shelves are mostly old, and the tiled and wood surround fireplace is inter-war. The door on the rear left leads to another bar with a couple of hatch-like counters in a part glazed partition wall to the rear of the servery. The room was extended back many years ago and the rear section has old dado panelling, tongue-and-groove ceiling, table skittles and fine views over the town and Cley Hill. Around 1960 a new lounge bar was created out of former outbuildings; it has ply-panelled walls and a counter front of a style seen widely in that era. Under the pub are remains of a 19th-century brewery and maltings and older vaults further below.

The rear bar (MSS)

Huish Episcopi

(On A372), TA10 9QT

01458 250494

Grade II listed

LPA: South Somerset

   (L, E)

Rose & Crown ('Eli's') ★

The Rose & Crown was known by this name by 1835 and is also affectionately called 'Eli's' after Eli Scott, grandfather of the present family members who run the pub. The simple Gothic windows suggest a rebuilding in the late-18th or early-19th centuries. Inside, its special feature is the sunken cellar area, a unique layout where customers freely wander in to order drinks or cross the pub. It has a stone-flagged floor and shelving with rare 'signal-lever' handpumps attached (see p.87). A series of small rooms surrounds it. One of these, the 'Men's Kitchen' (cf Globe, Appley) front right, was once a male preserve and has an old cast-iron range – such sex discrimination became illegal in 1976. Another historic room is the 'Piano Room' at the front in the middle of the building and with direct access to the serving area. To the left are two rooms brought into use; the front one was the family parlour and the rear was created in 1984 on the site of the outside gents'. A skittle alley occupies a separate building to the rear right of the pub; this is also the venue for Elderflowers Food Co-operative every Friday from 5pm to 7pm, selling locally produced, mostly organic, food at keen prices.

The cellar where customers freely wander in to order drinks or cross the pub

Kelston

Bath Road (A 431), BA1 9AQ
01225 423032
www.oldcrownkelston.com
Grade II listed
LPA: Bath & North East Somerset
 🍴 (L, E)

The public bar with a rare set of cash register handpumps

Old Crown ☆

This late-18th-century coaching inn has two small historic bars, both with flagstone floors, Victorian bar counters, stone fireplaces, dado panelling and fixed seating. The lounge bar (which was once a mortuary) has a notable bar-back fitting that moves to access the cellar. Fine heavy-carved settles can be found throughout the pub. The rarity here is the set of cash-register handpumps (in the public bar). Until recently, these were the only ones in regular use but they have now been joined by a renovated set at the Prince of Wales, Holcombe Regis, Devon and also one at a Kent micro-pub. Off the lounge, the small dining room was brought into use in recent years. Pity about the ubiquitous gastro-grey plain now liberally applied to old wooden surfaces.

Keynsham

93 Temple Street, BS31 1ER
Grade II Listed
LPA: Bath & North East Somerset
🍺

Ship Inn ☆

Late-17th-century pub with unusual stone mullioned windows at the front. The entrance passage, with old panelling and colourful tiled floor, was reduced to its present size in 1996 and the doors with 'Jug & Bottle' on the glass moved to enable staff to serve the left-hand room. To the right is the public bar, a long room with some of the finest bar fittings in North Somerset – an impressive long carved bar-back with barley-twist columns, mirrored sections and a significant part of surviving lower shelving; also a fine early-20th-century counter and dado panelling with old narrow benches attached along the outer wall. The right-hand part saw alterations in the 1950s, including the small brick fireplace, but these detract little from a very fine room.

The right-hand public bar (MSS)

Left of the lobby is a small lounge, which changed in 1996 when a new bar counter and the big stone fireplace were added, but the dado panelling is old. A short passage leads to a further room with a gallery which was created in 1996 from a former stable.

Midsomer Norton
The Island, BA3 2HQ
01761 418270
the-white-hart-public-house-
business-site
Grade II listed
LPA: Bath & North East Somerset

White Hart ☆

An excellent late-Victorian pub built of local stone and retaining its old layout of public bar, snug (formerly the lounge) and off-sales. The entrance lobby has an old settle and jug and bottle hatch, still used for service to customers drinking in the lobby and passageway. The passage turns at right-angles with a couple of tables under the staircase. On the left is a good vestibule entrance with full-height

The little-altered public bar

panelling and double doors leading to the public bar, which is hardly altered from when it was built. Its features include an original counter (the unusual curve at the far end made in 1985 when new gents' toilets were added), the original bar-back with slender columns between the shelving, Victorian tiled and cast-iron fireplace with marble surround, timber panelled dado with fixed benches attached and a partition wall on the jug and bottle side. Even the pot shelf above the counter is old! The snug on the right of the entrance retains its original panelled dado with some wall benches attached, and an old cast iron fireplace with mirrored surround above. The new lounge to the rear was created in 1985 and is a combination of a former beer store, which was roughly situated where the present servery stands, and a private lounge.

A skittle alley on the right in the far end of the former beer store was probably first introduced in the 1950s or 1960s. Ask the licensee to show you the old spittoon more recently used as an ashtray.

Nailsea

West End, BS48 4DE
01275 856910
Not listed
LPA: North Somerset
  (L Wed–Fri)

Blue Flame A basic cottage-style beerhouse still with three rooms., the front two being little-altered for fifty years . The atmospheric room at the front right is served through a wide arch opening with casks of beer and cider on a stillage beyond. Most of the fittings here are from the 1960s including lino floor, ply-panelled counter front, old shelves for a bar-back, wall cupboards, stone fireplace (with old full-height panelling each side) and assorted benches. The front-left room has a 1950s fireplace and a couple of old benches. In 2015 the back area of the pub was opened out with a counter replacing a hatch. On the rear left, steps down lead to 'The Shed' created in 2015 which has a stone floor and table skittles ready to play.

The Blue Flame still retains its outside toilets

Porlock

Porlock Hill (A39), TA24 8QD
01643 862507
www.shipinnporlock.co.uk
Listed Grade II
LPA: West Somerset
 (L, E)

Ship ('Top Ship') ☆

A 16th/17th-century thatched inn enlarged in the early/mid-19th century. It is called 'Top Ship' to avoid confusion with the Ship at Porlock Wier, nearer the coast. The 'must see' here is the tiny original boarded bar left of the entrance which has a red and black quarry-tiled floor, basic bench seating attached to old panelling on the wall, an old stone fireplace in one corner with a log burner and just a couple of tables, The counter was brought from a bank some 60 years ago (hence the height); mounted on it is a rare set of four handpumps on a pewter base. The bar-back shelves are probably less old than the rest of the fittings. Two further rooms to the right have been knocked into one and have some old dado panelling and benches. A rear bar and restaurant have been added in recent years and there is also a function room and a games room.

The rear bar with casks on stillage

Priddy

Old Bristol Road, BA5 3AR
01749 672275
Not listed
LPA: Mendip
   (L, E)

Hunter's Lodge ☆

A farmhouse from around 1780, still with 26 acres of land attached, and in the same family ownership for 102 years, with licensee Roger Dors here since 1946. Situated at a crossroads east of the village, nothing has changed at the pub since 1964. Originally, a passage ran from the front door to the rear with a public bar front left, a lounge front right and, rear left, a room with a bar counter across the gap between the two rooms. A hatch for off-sales was then added, quarter-circle counters were introduced and the rear-right room, formerly private quarters, was brought into use. The front-left public bar has a flagstone floor, a classic 1950s tiled fireplace, a quarter circle bar counter and dado panelling

The tiny original bar

with bare bench seating attached. At the back, across the gap where the original counter was situated, is another small room with a flagstone floor, another 1964 counter, and a settle under an old inglenook. The lounge on the right has a quarter-circle panelled counter, a small stove and a wood surround fireplace from the 1960s. The bare seating and bar-back shelving situated either side of the off-sales hatch were added in 1964. Rear right is another bar with a terrazzo tiled floor, a 1960s curved counter, and dado panelling with bare bench seating attached.

Weston-super-Mare
43 Upper Church Road, BS23 2DY
07538 753350
Not listed
LPA: North Somerset

Criterion Late-Victorian building which evolved from a lodging house into a pub. The main interest lies in the impressive old curved counter and the fine mirrored bar-back. The interior has been opened out and extended at the back; the counter in the latter area is a later copy of that in the main bar. The door currently in use formerly accessed an off-sales.

The bar fittings are little-altered since it became a pub

If in the area, the **Bell Inn, Banwell**, BS29 6BL is worth a look for its very old counter and moulded framed ceilings.

Witham Friary, BA11 5HF
01749 850742
Grade II listed
LPA: Mendip

The flagstone-floored corridor and glazed servery

Seymour Arms ★

Owned by the Douel family since 1943, this pub is a wonderful survival. It was purpose-built, along with farm buildings around 1866 for the Duke of Somerset's estate, and thus shows how rural pubs were often combined with farming and other functions (see Hunter's Lodge, p. 95). The farm was sold in 1980. The pub has a plain but dignified exterior with a splendid wrought-iron inn sign on one corner and a surprisingly spacious interior of two rooms astride a large flagstoned corridor. The latter leads up to a glazed servery with horizontally sliding windows, within which is a bank of four (unused) brass taps and a number of built-in drawers, all no doubt dating from the building of the pub. The ground floor cellar is off to the left. The main public bar is front left and has simple bench seating and service by a hatch from the 'cellar'. To the right is the 'Commercial Room'. The only major change has been the addition of inside toilets in 1981. The adjective 'timeless' was invented for places like this. As much cider as beer is sold – something which would have been true in most rural Somerset pubs until quite recently. *(A very similar pub, the Somerset Arms at Maiden Bradley, over the Wiltshire border, complete with farm buildings, was also built for the Seymour estate, but is now completely modernised.)*

97

What's in a Room Name (or Number)?

Not that long ago, all but the smallest pubs had two or more rooms. These were differentiated in terms of their ambience, clientele and, as a consequence, prices. The way a Victorian or Edwardian pub was laid out can be easily understood, despite the opening-up which has taken place, with a visit to the Cricketers, Bournemouth, Dorset (p.52). Here, the surviving window glass with room names includes 'smoking room', 'public bar', 'bottle & jug', 'private bar' and 'office'. What is now the lounge was originally the billiard room.

The most straight-forward pub room was the **public bar** where the beer was a little cheaper but the fixtures and fittings fairly basic. Better-appointed rooms went by a bewildering variety of names. **Private bars** did not require membership but were smaller than the public and the name suggests occupancy by regulars who knew one another. Rooms still bearing this title can be found at the London Inn, Padstow, Cornwall (p.22), the

Cricketers, Bournemouth

Cricketers, Bournemouth (p.52), and the Nova Scotia, Bristol (p.67). Where such rooms were particularly small, they were known as **snugs**. Also on the small side are **parlours**, which, generally, have a particular air of privacy about them; the Bridge Inn, Topsham, Devon (p.48) has an especially choice example.

The **lounge** or **saloon/saloon bar** tended to be larger and you could expect carpets, panelling and even waiter service.

The **smoking room/smoke room** is an odd one, suggesting it was where people could smoke.

Cricketers, Bournemouth

However, since smoking was allowed throughout the pub (until the recent smoking ban), a literal meaning makes no sense. These rooms were normally smaller than the public bar or lounge and the idea may have evolved to identify a haven where a chap (and it would

Old Green Tree, Bath, showing the room numb[er]

have been a chap) could take his ease in the way he would have done in a gentleman's smoking room. The Cricketers, Bournemouth (p.52) retains evidence of having had such a room.

Another paradoxical name is the **tap room**. You might assume this was where drinks were dispensed but old plans of pubs, and the layouts of those with surviving tap rooms, indicate otherwise. It may be that the name did once describe what took place in this room but, as with many aspects of pub lore, the title has become subverted. The suggestion we've heard that regulars would tap a coin to summon service seems fanciful given the (sometimes considerable) distance between tap rooms and serveries. Anyway, the South West's most renowned tap room is that at Tucker's Grave, Faulkland, Somerset (p.88) where the lettering on the door is reckoned to be at least 200 years old, making it the oldest in the country. It was preserved by being covered over for many years by a screwed-on plate.

Pubs often had a **club room** or **assembly room** used for meetings or other private gatherings, generally on an upper floor. The suitably-inscribed doors which led to one such can be seen at the Victoria

Cricketers, Bournemouth

Unusual room name at the Victoria, Oldfield Park, Bath (closed at the time of writing)

Globe, Appley

Cricketers, Bournemouth

Hotel, Bath (p.111, though the pub was closed at the time of writing.)

The rooms mentioned are the most common for traditional pub rooms, but many others exist. **Commercial rooms** are regularly found in the north but the Railway Inn, St Agnes, Cornwall (p.28) has one; the name suggests a location for business dealings and the village was a centre for the quarry industry. Alternatively, they may have been intended as areas for commercial travellers and their ilk to hang out. The right-hand room at the Seymour Arms, Witham Friary, Somerset (p.97), also has this appellation. **Men's kitchen** is a real

rarity but Somerset has two – at the Rose & Crown, Huish Episcopi (p.91), and the Globe, Appley (p.79). They were presumably male preserves but how much cooking went on is unknown – though the one in the Rose & Crown does have an old cast-iron range. Both the Larkhall (p.82) and the Star (p.81) in Bath have a **glass room** but the origin of the name is obscure.

Rare wording at the Star, Bath

Finally, you might, as at (again) the Cricketers, Bournemouth, see '**office**' on a pub door (another pub with an office is the Nova Scotia, Bristol (p.67), accessed through the bar-back.) As the name implies, this would lead to a publican's

admin area rather than a public space. In London especially, offices were often glazed-in areas behind the bar but down in the South West, more discrete arrangements applied.

You will sometimes find numbers on or above a door within a pub. There used to be (probably until the 1960s) a legal requirement on licensees to 'make entry' of their premises with HM Customs and Excise so they could check that the premises complied with the law. The process included listing all the rooms used both for the storage and the consumption of alcohol. At the Old Green Tree, Bath (p.80), the lounge has a figure '1', the public bar has a '2', the smoke room a '3' and there is a '4' on the cellar door. Although rooms might be identified by their names, they were more often denoted by numbers – a few of which can still be seen. The ancient 'Tap Room' lettering at Tucker's Grave, Faulkland, Somerset (p.88), no doubt predates the numbering requirement.

Railway, St Agnes

The oldest room wording in the country at the Tucker's Grave, Faukland

Pub listings **Wiltshire**

Gloucestershire & Bristol

Marlborough

Broughton Gifford

Devizes

Easton Royal

Bradford-on-Avon Poulshot

Pewsey

Somerset

Kilmington

Salisbury

Alderbury

Ebbesbourne Wake

Hamptworth

Dorset

N

0   10km

Alderbury
Old Road, SP5 3AR
01722 710263
Grade II listed
LPA: Wiltshire
🍺 🍴 (L, E)

Green Dragon A 15th-century hall house which in due course became a pub and retains much from an inter-war refurbishment. The inner lobby has a red tiled floor and an off-sales window. A latch door on the right leads to the lounge where the 1930s features include a fielded panelled counter, bar-back fitting and brick fireplace – the thatch over the servery is a modern addition. Old dado panelling, painted brown, covers the front wall where fixed seating was removed to create more dining space; dado panelling elsewhere is wood stained. The left-hand public bar was originally just the front room but has been opened up to incorporate the room behind, hence the bar now being U-shaped. The small bar counter is inter-war as are the brick fireplace and dado panelling. The back section has a hatch/doorway for staff and service to the garden. Retains outside gents'. The inn featured in Dickens' Martin Chuzzlewit as the Blue Dragon.

The left-hand public bar (MSS)

Ashley, Bradford-on-Avon

Ashley Road, BR15 1RT
01225 862137
www.dogandfoxinn.com
Not listed
LPA: Wiltshire

  (L, E)

Service is via a hatch in the right-hand lounge bar (MSS)

Dog & Fox ☆

Stone-built, edge-of-town pub with an unspoilt public bar and extended lounge. The lobby has bare seating and beyond the front door is a tiny area with a blue brick floor in front of a hatch-split door for staff, formerly accessing the off-sales with a new bar top, and old painted dado panelling. A door on the left leads to a splendid small public bar with a bare wood floor, very old dado panelling painted blue with bare benches attached, a baffle/draught screen by the door and window seating. The central servery has a counter front with a ribbed hardboard frontage which may have replaced a hatch in the 1950s; the bar-back shelving was added in the late 1990s to replace shelves on a mirrored backing. Note the old meat store on the rear wall. On the right, through a part glazed door, is the two-part lounge with old dado panelling painted deep red. Service is via a hatch with two open small windows and Formica top. The old stone fireplace has signs of a bread oven. Curtains divide the lounge from the dining room, occupying a modern extension.

The small public bar (MSS)

Broughton Gifford

The Common, SN12 8LX
01225 782309
www.bellonthecommon.co.uk
Not listed
LPA: Wiltshire

  (L, E; not Mon, Tue)

Bell on the Common Of most interest here is the Copper Lounge Bar, accessed from the left-hand entrance and named for the curved copper-topped counter, with front covered in copper panels, a copper hood above the fireplace and copper-topped tables, all from around 1959. Behind is a modern restaurant. The public bar to the right also dates mostly from 1959, having been two rooms before that; another copper hood adorns the old fireplace. A separate pool room has full-height wall panelling and bare wall benches. The bowling green at the back is owned by Wadworths brewery and leased to the bowling club.

101

Bell on the Common:
the aptly named Copper Bar

Devizes

20 St. John's Street, SN10 1BT

01380 725426

www.wadworth.co.uk/find-a-pub/
lamb-inn-devizes

Grade II listed

LPA: Wiltshire

The bare-boarded public bar (MSS)

Lamb Brick and timber-framed pub dating from 1630 which is remarkably unspoilt considering its town centre location. A flagstoned entrance passage leads to the courtyard. On the left, the bare-boarded public bar is now one U-shaped room around an old servery; the panelling on the counter front was transferred to the ceiling (!) in 1996 and replaced by part of a 17th-century French church door. The full-height wood panelling with bench seating is of some age. At least one other partition wall formerly separated the rear section; the existence of two pre-war medieval-style stone fireplaces confirms this. The stained glass panels by the entrance are a 1996 addition. The rear area has old dado panelling with an old bench attached plus church pews. Up one step at the back of the bar, a plain room is used for pool. To the right of the passage is the Shoot Room – the blocked-up door was once the main pub entrance. Of special interest here is the circular opening in the south wall with a metal tube extending 43 feet downwards with a target at the end. It is said to have been installed in 1903 to train locals with guns as Germany re-armed and is still used by the pub's team in the local small-bore rifles league.

Easton Royal

Easton Road (B3087), SN9 5LR
01672 810216
www.thebrucearms.net
Not listed
LPA: Wiltshire

The simply-appointed public bar

Bruce Arms ('The Gammon') ★

This superbly traditional roadside pub lies nearly a mile west of the village. Built around 1850, it was in the same family hands from 1918 to 1993, when licensee Rose Raisey died at the age of 87 – her picture is in the public bar. At the entrance is a small snug with a counter and red and black quarry-tiled floor. To its right, the simply-appointed public bar has a red brick floor and scrubbed Victorian tables and benches. The counter is thought to be from a refit in the 1930s, a date which would accord well with the brick fireplace. The basic shelving in the servery is probably later. Rose's kitchen has been brought into public use and, further on, a 1996 extension serves as a games room. The lounge, to the left of the entrance, has a small hatch to the servery and is furnished with domestic sofas and chairs, along with a piano bought for Rose when she was 13. The pub is nicknamed 'the Gammon', supposedly because it stood opposite a pub of that name which burned down about 1830. Large campsite at rear. Open from 5pm Mon to Fri.

Ebbesbourne Wake, SP5 5JF
01722 780474
www.thehorseshoe-inn.co.uk
Not listed
LPA: Wiltshire
 ¶¶ (L, E)

Horseshoe ☆

Brick-built 18th-century village pub with three small rooms. The front door takes you into a small cross-passageway with a screened servery beyond. A door in the servery for staff would have doubled up as an off-sales and there are (formerly sliding) windows displaying sweets for sale. Within the servery is an old stillage with a row of beer casks; above are old shelves, with another over the front partition wall of the servery. A small room on the left has some dado panelling with bench

103

The main right-hand bar with casks on stillage

seating attached and a hatch with rising panels in the open position (on the servery side it looks like a display case). Right of the passage through an old door is the main room with a lapped-wood 1950s counter, a large brick 1950s fireplace, dado panelling and farm tools and implements on the walls and fireplace. A further small room on the far right, formerly a private sitting room, was brought into use in the 1980s, but note the outline of the former bread oven in the brickwork passageway, dating from when the premises was a bakery many years ago. Further right still is a small conservatory extension. The pub retains its outside gents' (modernised) on the far right side of the pub.

Hamptworth

Hamptworth Road, SP5 2DU
01794 390302
www.restaurantwebx.com/
CuckooInn
Grade II listed
LPA: Wiltshire
🍺 🍴 (L)

Cuckoo Built as two cottages around 1800 of brick with thatched roof, this was a pub by 1901. The right-hand lounge area was the village shop until the 1960s and now accommodates the main entrance. The small bar counter is of no great age and the bench seating is recent. A doorway leads to the public bar (originally the main bar) where, again, the furnishings were acquired not long ago. Through a gap is the rear bar with red floor tiles, benches, tables and chairs of varying vintages and a Victorian cast-iron fireplace. The servery, which it shares with the public bar, has a counter in a distinct 1950s style and a bar-back with a mix of old and new shelving. The fourth room, rear left, was originally the kitchen with a fireplace and seating of more recent vintage. The building has no foundations or damp course so the dado match-boarding throughout was installed in 2000 to cover up and help prevent rising damp problems. Note the tiled mural commemorating the pub cricket tour of 1932.

The servery has a 1950s bar counter front (MSS)

Kilmington

(On B3092), BA12 6RP
01985 844263
www.theredlionkilmington.co.uk
Not listed
LPA: Wiltshire
 (L, E [Thu–Sat])

Red Lion Much fabric in this 15th-century building remains from a 1930s refit. This is when the panelled bar counter (inlaid with industrial lino which was refreshed a few years ago) was installed along with the modest bar-back fitting and the brick fireplaces; the settle has been here since around 1900. Completing the picture we have some old dado panelling and both window and fixed seating. Rear right, through a double door-width gap, is the back bar. This was, until the 1980s, a small room used for meetings but in 2013 it was enlarged by combining it with the licensee's sitting room. The pub is owned by the National Trust.

The main bar in this National Trust owned pub (MSS)

Marlborough

The Parade, SN8 1NE
01672 512668
www.thelambinnmarlborough.com
Not listed
LPA: Wiltshire
 (L)

Lamb An old coaching inn, purchased by Wadworths in 1905 – the plan from this time is on the wall. The fine bar-back in the front bar, with shelves held up by slender columns on a mirrored back, is probably from that time while the counter and parquet floor look inter-war. Wooden casks are stillaged behind the bar but, sadly, these are now just for show since Wadworths recently stopped supplying beer 'from the wood'. Gaps either side of the fireplace lead to a room also with an inter-war counter and attractive bar-back plus old fixed seating. A final 1930s counter is in the small rear room.

The bar back – the wooden casks are now just for show (MSS)

105

Pewsey

37–39 Ball Road, SN9 5BL
01672 562495
Grade II listed
LPA: Wiltshire

Coopers Arms The bare-boarded L-shaped main bar, wrapped round an irregularly shaped servery, originally comprised the public area in this 17th-century timber-framed brick building. The panelled counter and mirrored bar-back, with delicate barley-twist columns, may date from around 1927 when the pub was recorded as 'fully licensed'. Sadly, the rear right wall has been removed with modern cabinets added which detracts somewhat. Old benches and some chunky rustic furniture populate the room – the small modern fireplace on the left suggests there was once a partition. A short passage down the left side leads to a dining room/lounge then up some steps is a pool room – both these came into public use quite recently.

The irregularly-shaped servery (MSS)

Poulshot

Poulshot Road, SN10 1RW
01380 828271
www.ravenpoulshot.co.uk
Grade II listed
LPA: Wiltshire

 (L, E)

Raven 17th-century timber framed building with a 19th-century extension. The left-hand door leads into a passage created by a floor-to-ceiling settle (with glazed panels on top), the public bar being through a gap between this and the servery. This small room has an old bar counter but the bar-back fitting is recent. Below it, wooden casks are stillaged but, as at the Lamb, Marlborough, no longer contain Wadworth's beer. Other features are the inter-war brick fireplace, old fixed seating and parquet floor. A small lounge on the right has a similar fireplace and service via a hatch. The dining room is a modern creation.

The old bar counter and rear of a high-backed settle

Salisbury

1–5 Minster Street, SN10 1RW

01722 411313

www.haunchpub.co.uk

Grade II listed

LPA: Wiltshire

 (L, E)

Haunch of Venison ★

A pub of great antiquity and character. Although mainly 15th-century (whence the mighty timbers inside), it was altered in the 18th and then had a still-surviving refit in 1909. Right of the lobby, a tiny room (sometimes referred to as the 'Ladies' Snug') has a black and white stone floor, panelled walls with benches attached and a rare pewter counter top. Mounted on this is a wooden arch with beautiful inlaid brasswork and plates naming the maker as 'H. Neale, Plumber, Salisbury'. It is adorned with ten taps to dispense spirits and fortified wines. Another bank of eight taps sits against the right-hand wall. Surviving sets of spirit cocks can be found in only four other UK pubs. Through a pair of narrow double doors, the public bar (or 'House of Commons') has more black and white flooring, panelled walls, benches (with cupboards below) and another pewter counter-top. Beer is dispensed from handpumps which, unusually, are situated on the bar-back. Up some steps, the 'House of Lords' has a low, beamed ceiling, panelled walls and an inglenook fireplace, besides which is a former bread oven containing a grisly, mummified hand (supposedly of a cheating card-player). Up more stairs, the restaurant is two rooms, the right-hand one extending into a 16th-century merchant's house.

The servery with a pewter bar top and rare set of spirit cocks

Haunch of Venison: the tiny snug

Salisbury

69 Brown Street, SP1 2AS
01722 327137
www.raidor.co.uk
Grade II listed
LPA: Wiltshire

 (E)

The front left area (MSS)

Rai d'Or According to Historic England, the building dates from the mid-16th century, though it has been much altered. The interior has been opened out into a single L-shaped room with bare floorboards and a large open fireplace; modern wooden screens break up the space into three areas. The Brown Street door leads, via a small vestibule, to the bar area where the counter has old wooden panels but the bar-back is modern. Along the back of the room is fixed bench seating and this, rather oddly, extends along the wall past the edge of the fireplace into a very small alcove. The other entrance, from Trinity Street, brings you to an area with an inter-war fireplace and some more bench seating. The establishment operates more as a Thai restaurant these days.

Closed Pubs

CAMRA surveys reveal that, at any one time, around 2,000 UK pubs are 'in limbo' – closed for the time being but not necessarily gone for ever. Needless to say, a number of South West pubs with important historic interiors fall into this category. We are hopeful that some at least will return to active service under owners who will appreciate the heritage value of their assets.

The following pubs would have featured in this guide had they been open at the time it was being prepared; the descriptions tell you what they were like when last open. You can check the current status of the pubs by visiting CAMRA's on-line pubs database WhatPub – **whatpub.com**

DEVON

Stockland
Honiton Road, EX14 9BS
01404 881198
Grade II listed
LPA: East Devon

The Kings Arms, Stockland has a rare ten-pin skittle alley

Kings Arms ☆
16th-century thatched country inn that appears little changed since a refit in around 1960. The Farmers Bar at the rear has stone walls, an old flagstone floor and dado panelling plus a counter and bar-back from the refit. At the front, a 500 year old oak screen separates two rooms. Left is a small bar with a refit-period counter and lower bar back shelves, a small stone fireplace and old dado panelling. The other room has an old stone fireplace and settles while the dining room, rear right also has a stone fireplace (with bread oven). The skittle alley in a modern extension on the left has the rare ten pin version.

Ampney St Peter, GL7 5SL
Grade II listed
LPA: Cotswold

Red Lion ★

An unspoilt rural classic with two rooms either side of a central corridor and one of those rare pubs with no bar counter – beer dispense was

via a pair of handpumps mounted against the back wall. In the public bar, customers sat around a central table and convivial conversation was inevitable. It closed in 2014 on the death of veteran licensee John Barnard. Attempts to obtain planning permission for conversion to residential have been rebuffed. The building has now been sold but the intentions of the new owners are not yet known.

The Red Lion, Ampney St Peter, closed for some time, has been sold and may re-open?

Bristol: St George
Blackworth Road, BS5 8AS
Not listed   LPA: Bristol

Three Crowns ☆

This large red-brick pub of 1904 retains some fine Edwardian bar fittings, notably the three-sectioned mahogany bar-back with mirrors, decorative capital and three small drawers. The old bar counter may have been shortened a little in recent times. Good vestibule entrance as well. Closed in 2018 when the owners went into liquidation. The Save the Three Crowns group has achieved Asset of Community Value registration and is fighting to get the pub re-opened. At the time of writing they were in negotiations with the estate agents regarding a possible sale.

The Three Crowns, Bristol, St George
closed in 2018 (Photo by Tim Belsten)

Bristol: St Philip's

1–2 West Street, BS2 0DF

0117 955 2316

Grade II listed   LPA: Bristol

Palace Hotel ☆

Well worth a visit to see the impressive arcading with round arched, twisted, hollow brass columns that originally ran all along the side wall. In the spandrels, glass roundels with an eagle are surrounded by a belt bearing the emblem 'Strength'. Until 1970 this was a one-roomed hotel reception/residents & public bar room but was then split in two by creating a division wall and a second small lounge bar to the left/rear. Whilst the lower section of the arcading still runs all along the wall into the second room, the top sections and twisted brass columns were moved at right angles and now are situated on the rear wall of the main bar.

The Palace Hotel, Bristol, St Philips is temporarily closed and expected to re-open

SOMERSET

Bath: Oldfield Park

Millmead Road, BA2 3JW

01225 425903

Not listed

LPA: Bath & North East Somerset

🍺 🍴 (L)

The Victoria Hotel, Oldfield Park, Bath is up for lease so may re-open soon

Victoria Hotel   The three-room layout in this 1897-built pub is intact, though there has been much tinkering and modernisation. The best room is the small lounge on the right separated from an L-shaped corridor by a timber screen with 1930s leaded glass. In the room, the stone fireplace and bar counter look to be from the 1950s/1960s. The central servery is much altered but has a good, if odd, 'gantry' in the middle. In the passage, narrow double doors with 'Club Room' panels lead upstairs to a room with a skittle alley.

Stop Press: a planning application has been submitted to convert the building to a children's nursery so the pub may have been lost by the time the book is published.

Taking it Home

Where did you last buy a drink to take home? Chances are it was a supermarket, perhaps a convenience store or maybe a high street drinks shop. It's hardly likely to have been down at your local pub. Up until around 50 years ago, though, it would have been a different story. Many pubs sold drinks of all kinds for customers to enjoy at home and very often there was special provision in the building's layout to cater for this. Legislation changed in the 1960s to enable supermarkets to sell alcohol freely and the rest is history. The 'offie' at the pub is now largely a thing of the past.

The off-sales at pubs went under a bewildering variety of names: off-sales (of course), jug and bottle (and vice versa), outdoor department, order department, jug department and so on. You can sometimes still see the old names fossilised in etched glass or doorplates.

Sometimes a bench was provided in the space in question, typically to cater for the person waiting to be served. At the Bridge, Shortwood, Bristol (p.74), some customers liked to drink in the former 'outdoor department' which was also used by children buying sweets. Sadly, it has recently

Cricketers, Bournemouth

Rare 'Jug Dept.' wording at the George, Bridport (MSS)

become a storage area but you can still see the part-glazed screens separating it from the bar.

Where there was no special enclosed small space for off-sales, there might be a hatch facing the front door or in a corridor. The South West has some good surviving examples though only one is now used (occasionally) for its original purpose. At the White Hart, Midsomer Norton, Somerset (p.93), you can still order through the old hatch if drinking in the lobby. The Lamb & Fountain, Frome, Somerset (p.90) also has a corridor hatch, retaining a sliding glazed window with display case above.

Frome also has the best-surviving off-sales – at the Crown (p.89). This occupies a tiny space between rooms either side of the central servery. Beyond twin doors are a Victorian counter and walls panelled to full height. It still sees a little use, though the biggest selling item is cigarette papers.

The old offies at the Corner House, Barnstaple (p.34) and Teign Brewery Inn, Teignmouth (p.48)

are now storage areas while that at the Devonport Arms, Paignton (p.44) has been converted to a small family room (presumably for small families). Off-sales hatches can be seen at the Hunters Lodge, Priddy, Somerset (p.95 a late example from 1964) and the Queens Head, Albaston, Cornwall (p.19).

However, is the off-licence (or at least 'off-sales') making a comeback? Several recently opened micropubs also sell bottles and cans to take away while some small breweries have tap rooms where you can sample the beer on site and/or purchase for home consumption. Most Wetherspoons outlets and some other pubs now have a 'bottle shop' (albeit this is more of a service than a physically separate area) encouraging you to buy bottles or cans. What goes round…

The off-sales hatch at the Lamb & Fountain, Frome (MSS)

The Selection Criteria for CAMRA's Inventories

CAMRA's inventories of historic pub interiors focus entirely on the **internal physical fabric** of pubs and what is **authentically old** inside them. In this context a pub's external architecture, fine though it may be, is a side issue.

National or regional significance?
The pubs that qualify for the National Inventory of Historic Pub Interiors (NI) must have outstanding attributes – either a high degree of internal intactness or, where there has been alteration, some truly exceptional features or rooms. Outstanding bars and pub-type rooms in other kinds of establishment, such as hotel bars, theatre bars or railway buffets, are also embraced. Rather less is expected of candidates for a regional inventory of historic pub interiors (RI), although they must retain a significant amount of genuine historic features and/or a good sense of their historic layout. Most pubs included on an RI will have some combination of both. Pub interiors of Some Regional Interest (SRI) will have experienced even more change but have historic rooms or features worthy of acknowledgement.

Age
The main focus of CAMRA's inventories is on pre-1939 interiors – fabric that is much as it was before the Second World War – but some later interiors that have survived unaltered, especially from before the mid-1960s (when the modern orgy of pub refitting and opening-out began in earnest) are now rare and have to be seriously considered too. There is, however, a need for more research to develop appropriate criteria for post-war pubs and CAMRA has recently assisted Historic England with an in-depth study of this largely unrecognised era for pubs. In the meantime, CAMRA is careful to restrict its present selections to clear cases that have special merit (exceptional merit, in the case of the NI). Interiors later than 1970 do not qualify at all for the inventories.

Historic pub fittings, features and plan-form
The emphasis is on items that reflect the premises' historic function **as a pub**, rather than inherited from some other (usually domestic) use of the building, although the line is not always easy to draw. Items of specific interest include such things as fixed settles or bench seating, bar fittings (counter, bar-back), screen partitioning, bell-pushes, dispense equipment and original toilets as well as fittings and décor purpose-designed for pubs (most famously by the Victorians and Edwardians, in decorative glass, joinery, plaster and ceramic work). If features like these survive in abundance, with little lost, the pub is a clear candidate for the NI.

The survival of historic layout is also a crucial factor in assessing NI candidates, but RI candidates too should retain sufficient for their original internal planning to be appreciated and understood. Where a pub has undergone modern extension, as so many have, this need not count against it providing the work has been sensitively done (preferably kept physically separate) and does not seriously compromise its 'historic core'.

The bottom line?
If all that's left is a couple of fixed benches and a bit of matchboard panelling in a largely opened-up pub, inclusion will not be justified as these are common-place and can be found in large numbers. Many pub interiors too still have a few old features like etched glass or tilework which are irreplaceable and a joy to behold but CAMRA has been cautious about developing plans for a nationally-led campaign to identify and catalogue them – the hope being that the inspiration for compiling 'local inventories' will take off at the local level itself. The work done by Sheffield Branch of CAMRA in identifying and describing such pubs in their area shows what a worthwhile exercise this can be.

Factual evidence and informed judgement
CAMRA's inventories set great store by including only what is genuinely old. This ought to be a matter of objective, provable fact and certainly the selections for the South West Regional Inventory have been authenticated wherever possible from documentary sources like original plans, building records or other archive material. However, where no such material exists, as is often the case, the truth is not always easy to establish. Oral testimony from licensees and older regulars can be an invaluable help but reliance often has to be placed on experience and informed judgement.

Glossary

Ale: originally a fermented malt liquor, made without the use of hops. The term has been effectively interchangeable with 'beer' for at least the last 200 years.

Alehouse: originally, a house selling ale/beer, but not wine or spirits.

Art Deco: a fashionable style between the two world wars in Europe and America. It relies on geometrical patterns and sleek lines. The name comes from the Exposition International des Arts-Décoratifs in Paris in 1924–5 which greatly enhanced its popularity.

Arts and Crafts: a late 19th-century English artistic and architectural movement that emphasised the value of handicraft and good design as against mass-production methods.

Balustrade: row of small posts or columns lining a staircase or raised area, topped with a rail.

Bar-back: shelving, sometimes very ornately treated and incorporating mirrors, at the rear of a servery.

Barrel: although widely used as a term for any size of cask, the term applies, strictly speaking, to a vessel containing 36 gallons. This used to be the standard size for beer casks until the mid-20th century. Today, the standard cask contains nine gallons and is properly termed a firkin.

Beer engine: a device for raising beer from the cellar, nearly always referring to a handpump.

Bell push: a button that activated an electric bell or a visual indicator when there was table service in the better-class rooms of many pubs.

Bottle and jug: see off-sales.

Brewers' Tudor: a style, especially popular between the world wars, which drew nostalgically upon the half-timbered architecture of the Tudor period (see the photo of the Waverley Arms, Weymouth on p.16).

Cellar: a room where casks are stored, usually, but not necessarily below ground.

Cider: fermented apple juice with a maximum legal alcohol content of 8.5% (above this it would be classed as a wine for duty purposes).

Club room: a room in many traditional pubs which was used for meetings. Often on the first floor.

Coaching inn: strictly, an inn on one of the main coaching routes, where horses would be changed and where passengers could obtain refreshment. Today, the term is applied indiscriminately to any inn, whether or not it was a calling-place for coaches.

Commercial room: a better-quality room where commercial travellers and better-off tradesmen could gather.

Dado: the lower part of a wall, often but not always below a rail and above a skirting board and also often wood-panelled.

Delabole: a huge slate quarry in Cornwall which provided the flooring for many local pubs.

Fielded panelling: a series of wooden panels with a raised or sunken square or rectangular central section.

The Ship Inn, Shaftesbury has a fielded panelled bar counter and red & cream quarry-tiled floor in lozenge patterns

Formica: a laminate product, very popular in the 1950s and 1960s for counter tops or other surfaces needing to be kept clean.

Free house: a pub not tied to a brewer, whose landlord is free to obtain beer from any source. The term is widely abused by modern pub companies, who do not brew themselves but insist that their tenants obtain beer from specified suppliers.

Gable: the portion of a wall, usually triangular, between the edges of intersecting roof pitches.

Gastropub: a late 20th-century term for a pub where the main emphasis is on sophisticated food.

Gothic: a style of architecture from the middle ages which saw a revival in Victorian times.

Gravity dispense: beer or cider served direct from the cask into the glass.

Handpump: the lever on the bar which operates a beer engine to draw beer from the cask in the cellar, and now universally regarded as the standard method of dispense for real ale (q.v.).

Herringbone: an arrangement of rectangular blocks used in flooring whose pattern resembles the bones of a fish such as a herring.

Hogshead: a cask containing 54 gallons.

Inglenook: a recess adjoining a fireplace.

Inn: a house offering accommodation and refreshment to travellers.

Jug and bottle: see off-sales.

Lapped wood: planks or boards which overlap each other.

Lapped wood bar front, Kings Arms, Wareham

Lounge (bar): the most comfortably furnished room in a public house. Beer was usually more expensive in the lounge bar.

Matchboarding: see tongued-and-grooved boarding

Off-sales: sales of drink for consumption off the premises: the term sometimes is applied to the place in the pub where the sales take place (which also goes by other names such as jug and bottle).

Oyster Bar: an area where oysters are (or were) served buffet-style. Oysters were once common inn food.

Parquet: geometric mosaic of wood pieces used for decorative effect in flooring.

Perry: similar to cider but made from fermented pear juice. Production has declined severely since the 19th century.

Pint: the standard measure for beer: 20 fluid ounces (an eighth of a gallon) or 568ml.

Pot-shelf: a shelf over a bar counter for housing glasses. They appear to be a late 20th-century development, and have profoundly and adversely affected the appearance of many pubs.

Portico: colonnaded porch or entrance to a building.

Private bar: a more select area than the public bar. The name implies occupancy by a group of regulars known to one another.

Pubco: a pub-owning company with no brewing interests. They arose out of the Beer Orders of 1989

Public bar: the most basic pub room (known sometimes simply as the bar) where drink was slightly cheaper than in the better rooms.

Publican's rustic: a term used in this book for a nostalgic style of pub-fitting that began between the world wars, emphasising a consciously rustic atmosphere with large amounts of chunky woodwork and rough surfaces.

Quarry tile: floor tiles, usually red and black, in square or lozenge patterns.

Real ale: a term coined in the early 1970s to describe traditional beer, which undergoes a secondary fermentation and conditioning in the barrel (hence 'cask-conditioned' as opposed to 'keg' beers, which are brewery-conditioned).

Saloon: a better class pub room.

Screeded floor: one comprised of concrete that has been levelled and flattened before finishing.

Servery: the area, almost always behind a bar-counter, from which drinks are dispensed.

Settle: bench-seating, often curved, with a medium to high back.

Settles at the Castle Inn, Lydford

Slatted: narrow, overlapping strips of wood.

Smoke room: a better class pub room. In former times, when smoking was not a social issue, there is no reason to suppose that smoking was restricted to this area. It is likely that, being better furnished that the public bar, the room was somehow associated with taking one's ease, as in the smoking room of country houses.

Snug: a small, intimate drinking space.

Spirit cock: a tap from which spirits were drawn; a row of them indicates that the spirits were stored in casks in a room above the bar.

Spittoon: A receptacle for spit but no doubt accumulating cigar and cigarette ends, ash and other small refuse.

Stillage: a framework on which casks are mounted or 'stillaged' ready for service. Probably the name arises because of the need for traditional beer to remain still for a period to allow it to clear before service.

Tap room: a common pub room, but not, as the name might imply, connected to or within which drink was served or stored.

Tavern: originally a drinking house serving expensive imported wine, as well as good-quality food.

Terracotta: very hard-wearing, unglazed pottery.

Terrazzo: Flooring consisting of small pieces of marble set in concrete, rubbed down and polished.

Tied house: a public house which is committed to taking a particular brewery's beers, either because it is owned or leased by that brewery, or because the owner has accepted a loan in exchange for selling those beers alone (the so-called 'loan-tie').

Tongue(d)-and-groove(d) boarding: in pubs, cheap panelling on walls and ceilings and consisting of boards with tongues cut along one edge and grooves in the opposite edge and which are then joined together.

Vestibule: a hall or passage between an entrance and the main interior of a building.

The stillage of casks at the Hunters Lodge, Priddy

Editors' Acknowledgements

This book would not have been possible without the great contributions from CAMRA colleagues, especially fellow members of the Pub Heritage Group (PHG).

We are especially grateful to Michael Schouten, Chris Witt and Richard Williams for their help with surveying pubs in the final stages of the book's preparation.

Geoff Brandwood helped enormously with his careful proof-reading of the text and his suggestions for additions and improvements; several of the articles are also variants on the originals that Geoff wrote for previous publications in this series.

Andrea Briers and Chris Rouse from the APPLE committee helped by adding to the cider article.

PHG also thanks Katie Button from CAMRA Books for her help and encouragement with the project and our designer, Dale Tomlinson, who, as always, has ensured that the book looks great and shows off the wonderful pubs it features to maximum advantage.

Final thanks go to all the CAMRA members in the South West and elsewhere who, over the years, have suggested pubs for inclusion and provided information about them.

Index

Page numbers in **bold** indicate illustrations

Books for pub & beer lovers

CAMRA Books, the publishing arm of the Campaign for Real Ale, is the leading publisher of books on beer and pubs. Key titles include:

Good Beer Guide 2020
Edited by ROGER PROTZ

Now in its 47th edition, the *Good Beer Guide* is fully revised and updated each year to feature 4,500 recommended pubs across the United Kingdom that serve the best real ale. The beer-lovers' bible is completely independent, with listings based entirely on evaluation by CAMRA members. The unique breweries section lists every brewery – micro, regional and national – that produces real ale in the UK, and their beers. This is the complete book for beer lovers and for anyone wanting to experience the UK's finest pubs.

£15.99   ISBN 978 1 85249 358 5   *Available September 2019*

Britain's Best Real Heritage Pubs *New Edition*
GEOFF BRANDWOOD

This definitive listing is the result of 25 years' research by CAMRA to discover pubs that are either unaltered in 70 years or have features of truly national historic importance. Fully revised from the 2013 edition, the book boasts updated information and a new set of evocative illustrations. Among the 260 pubs, there are unspoilt country locals, Victorian drinking palaces and mighty roadhouses. The book has features describing how the pub developed and what's distinctive about pubs in different parts of the country.

£9.99   ISBN 978 1 85249 334 9

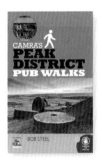

Peak District Pub Walks
BOB STEEL

CAMRA's *Peak District Pub Walks* has been tempting people into the magnificent dales, hills, and inns of the national park for over a decade. Now fully revised, this practical, pocket-sized guide will direct you to some of the best walks and finest pubs the Peak District has to offer. The 24 walking routes plus 3 cycle trails in the book combine stunning landscape, fascinating industrial heritage and some of the best real-ale pubs in the region. Ordnance Survey route maps and useful information such as travel and pub details and timing tips will help you make the best of your trips.

£12.99   ISBN 978 1 85249 353 0

The Pub Manifesto
JAMES DOWDESWELL

Twenty-one pubs close per week in the UK. Award-winning stand-up and pub aficionado James Dowdeswell – who grew up in a West Country pub – believes humour is the best way to make the plight of the pub public and to generate a response. To source the roots of the problem and to help crystallise what makes the perfect pub, James dissects, discusses and waxes lyrical on every aspect of pub culture. Dowdeswell's conversational prose style means reading this book is like sitting down with the author and discussing your ultimate pub over a beer.

£12.99   ISBN 978 1 85249 355 4

Order these and other CAMRA books online at **www.camra.org.uk/books**, *ask your local bookstore, or contact*: CAMRA, 230 Hatfield Road, St Albans, AL1 4LW. *Telephone* 01727 867201

Join CAMRA today

CAMRA, the Campaign for Real Ale, is an independent not-for-profit, volunteer-led consumer group. We promote good-quality real ale and pubs, as well as lobbying government to champion drinkers' rights and protect local pubs as centres of community life.

CAMRA has over 190,000 members from all ages and backgrounds, brought together by a common belief in the issues that CAMRA deals with and their love of good-quality British beer. From just £26.50 a year, you can join CAMRA and enjoy the following benefits:

- Award-winning, quarterly *BEER* magazine and monthly *What's Brewing* newspaper
- Free or reduced entry to over 180 beer festivals
- £30 worth of CAMRA real ale* vouchers
- Access to the Real Ale Discount Scheme, where you receive discounts on pints at over 3,500 participating pubs nationwide
- Learning resources to help you discover more about beer and brewing
- The opportunity to campaign for great real ale, cider and perry, and to save pubs under threat from closure
- Discounts on CAMRA books including our best-selling *Good Beer Guide*
- Social activities in your local area and exclusive member discounts online.

Whether you're a dedicated campaigner, a beer enthusiast looking to learn more about beer, or you just love to meet up with friends in your local, make sure to join the beer movement today!

Join the campaign at
www.camra.org.uk/joinus

CAMRA, 230 Hatfield Road, St Albans, Herts AL1 4LW.
Tel: **01727 798440**   Email: **camra@camra.org.uk**

Rates and benefits are subject to change.
*real ale, cider and perry, subject to terms and conditions.

Campaign
for
Real Ale